CREEPY KAWAII COLORING BOOK FOR KIDS

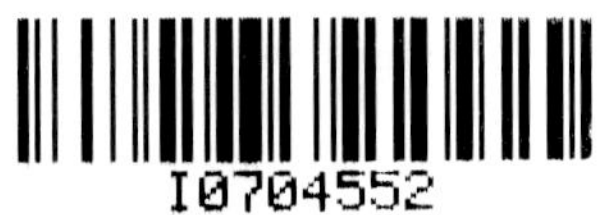

Belongs to:

Name: ....

Address: ....

....

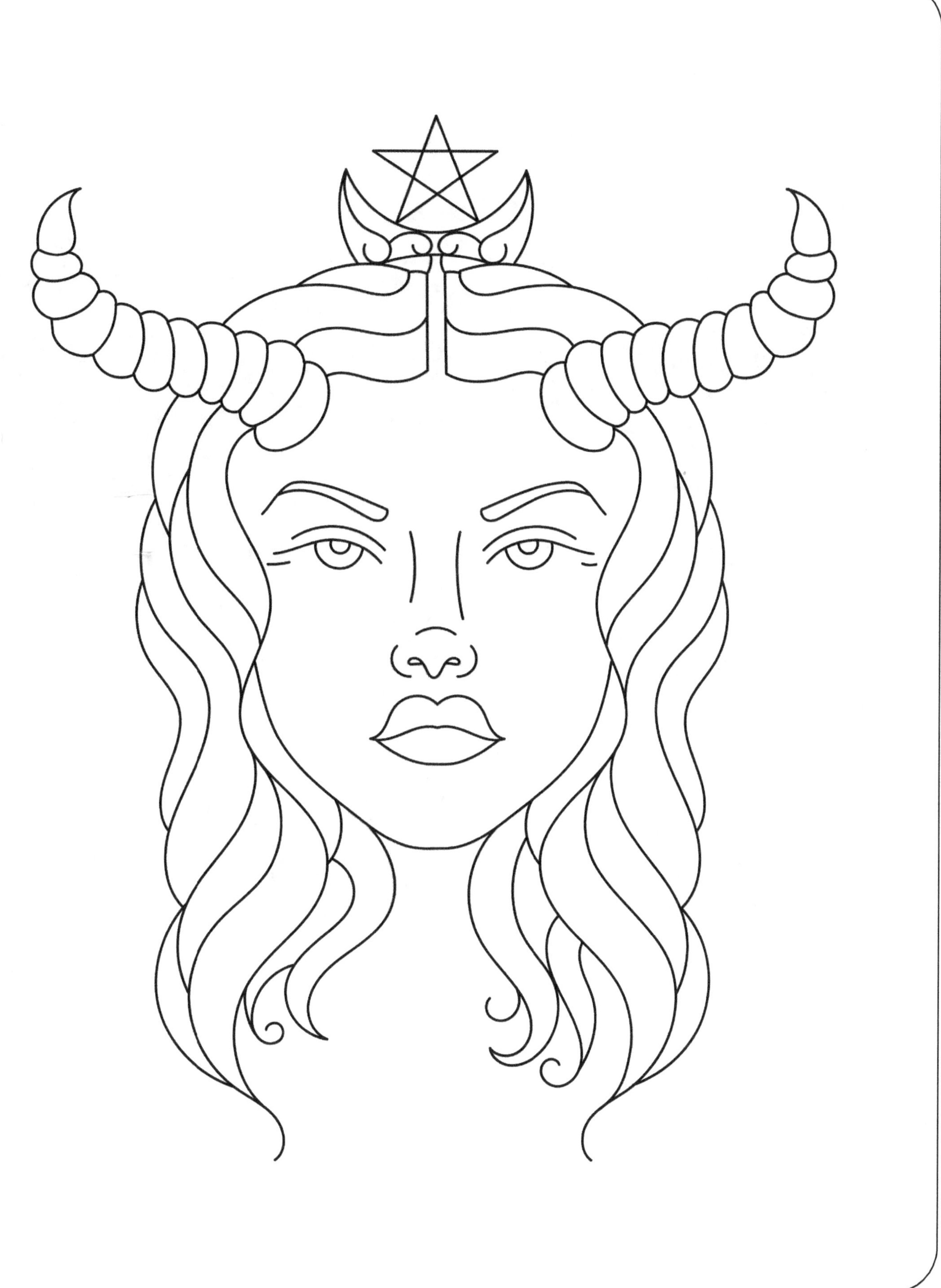

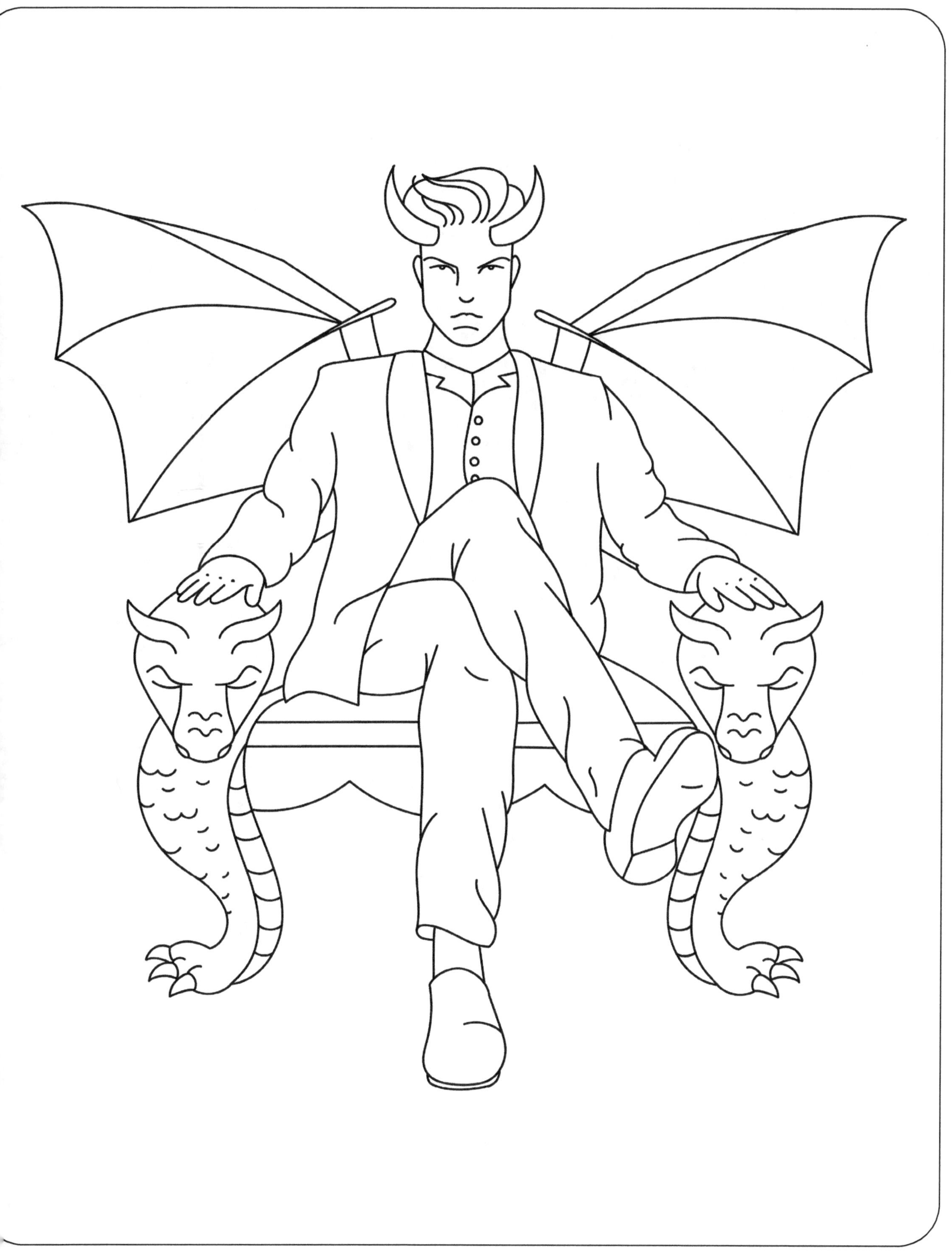

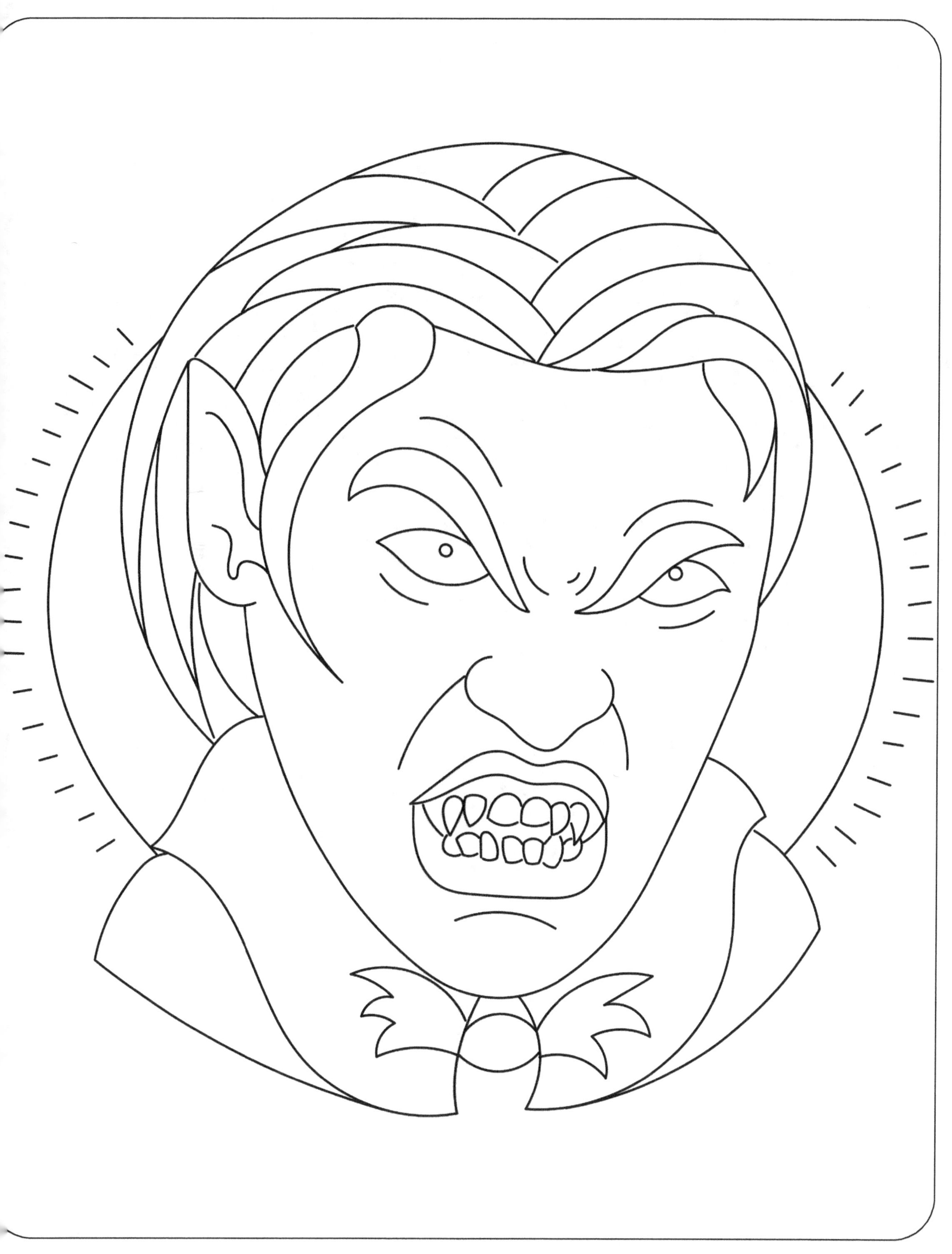

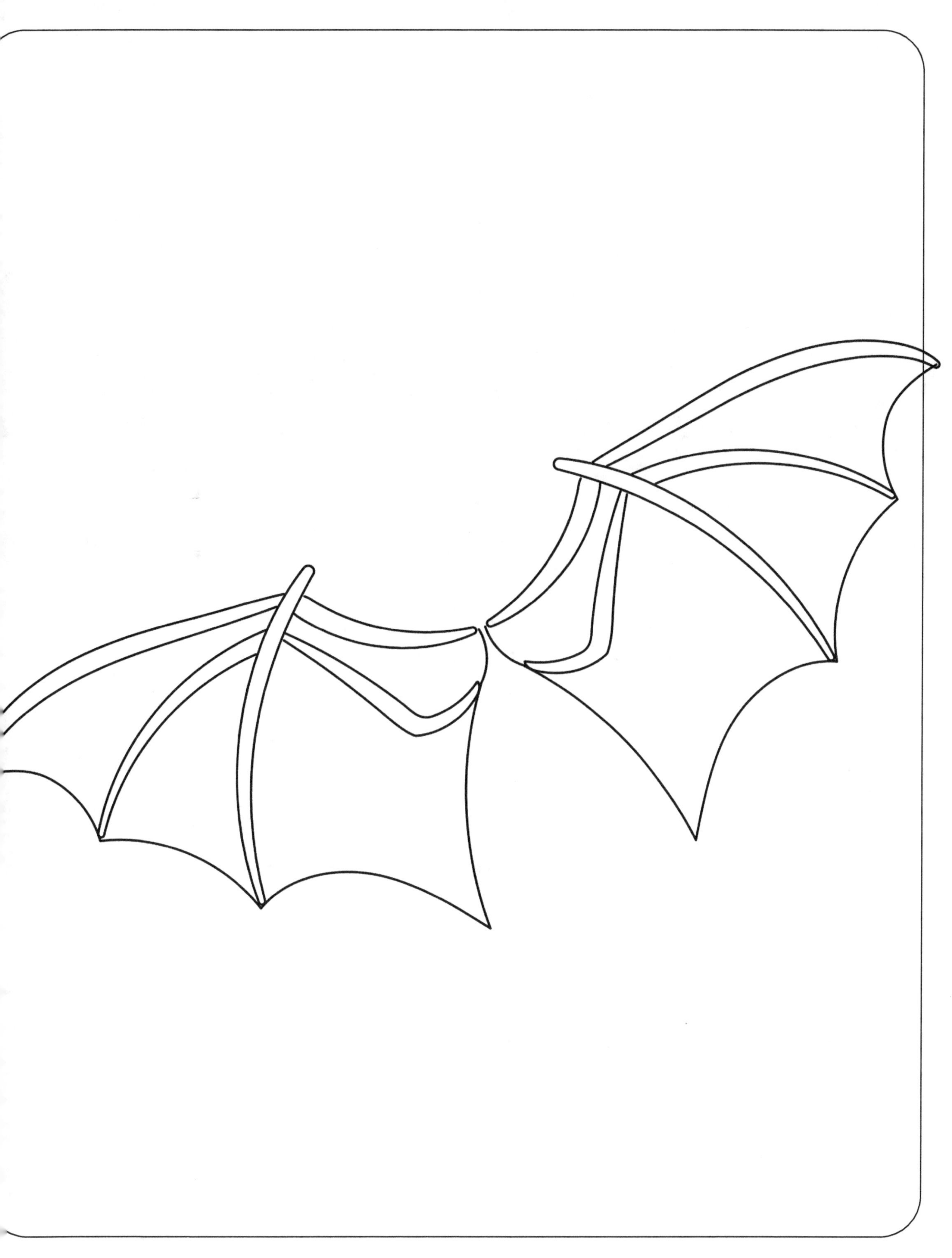

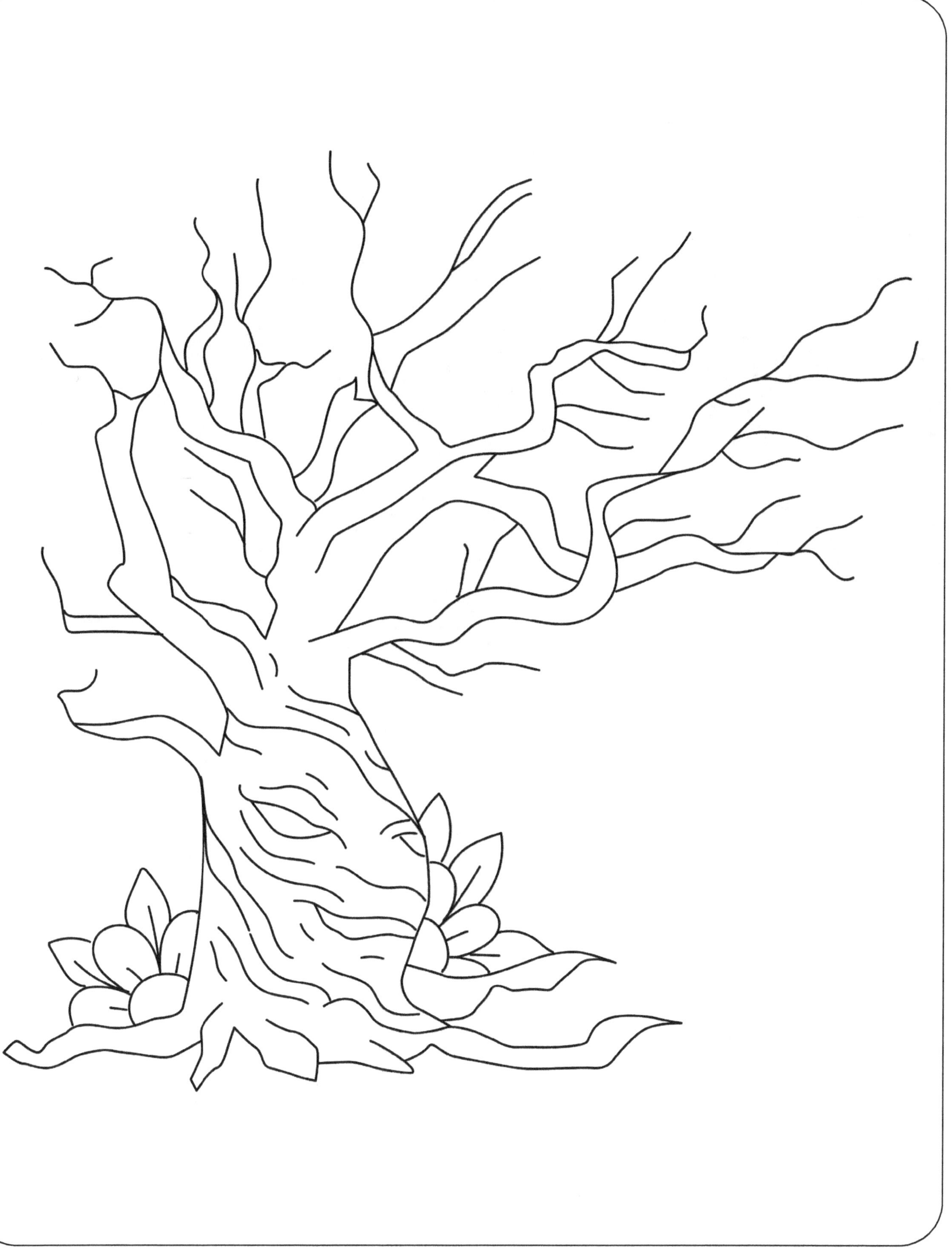

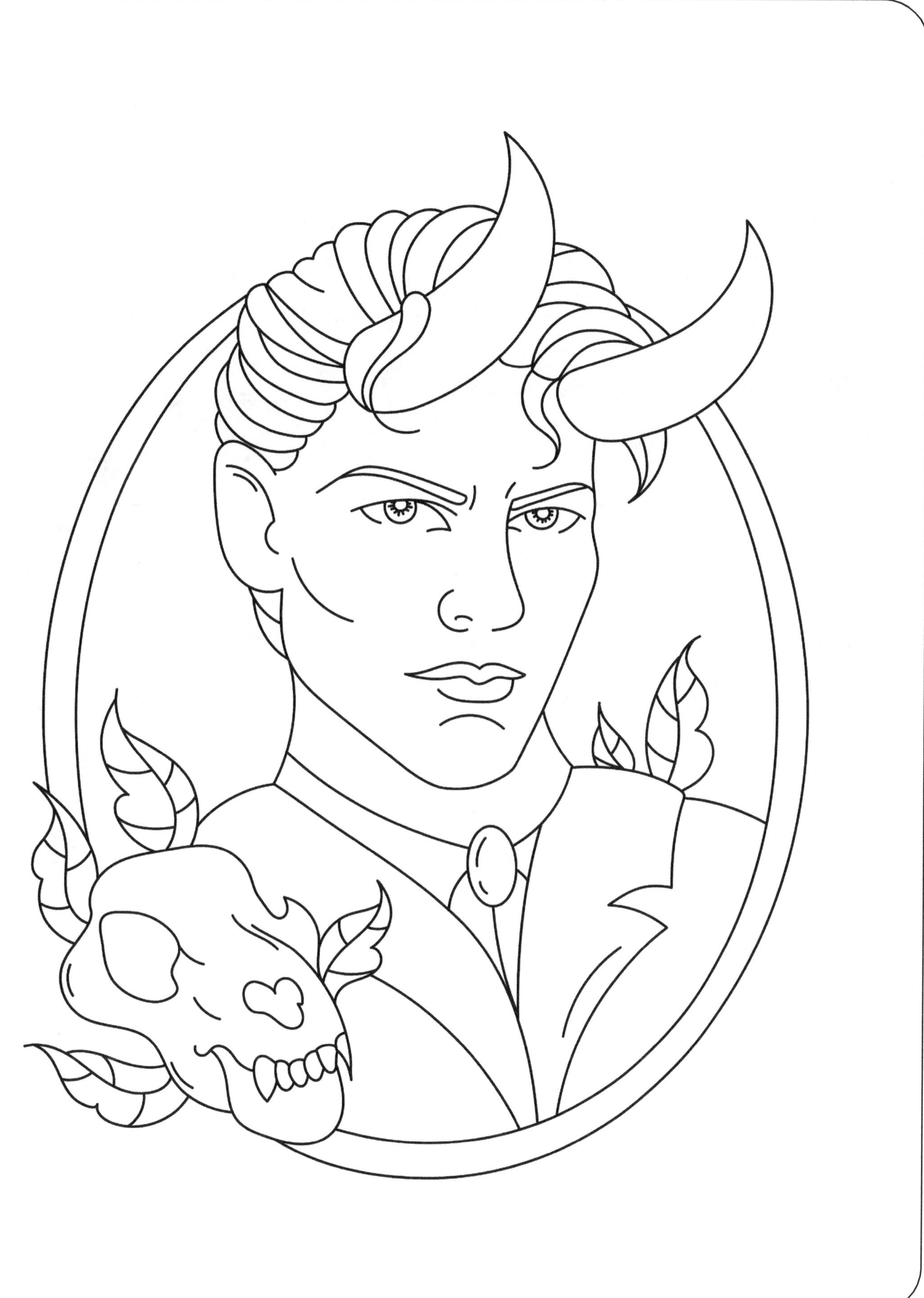

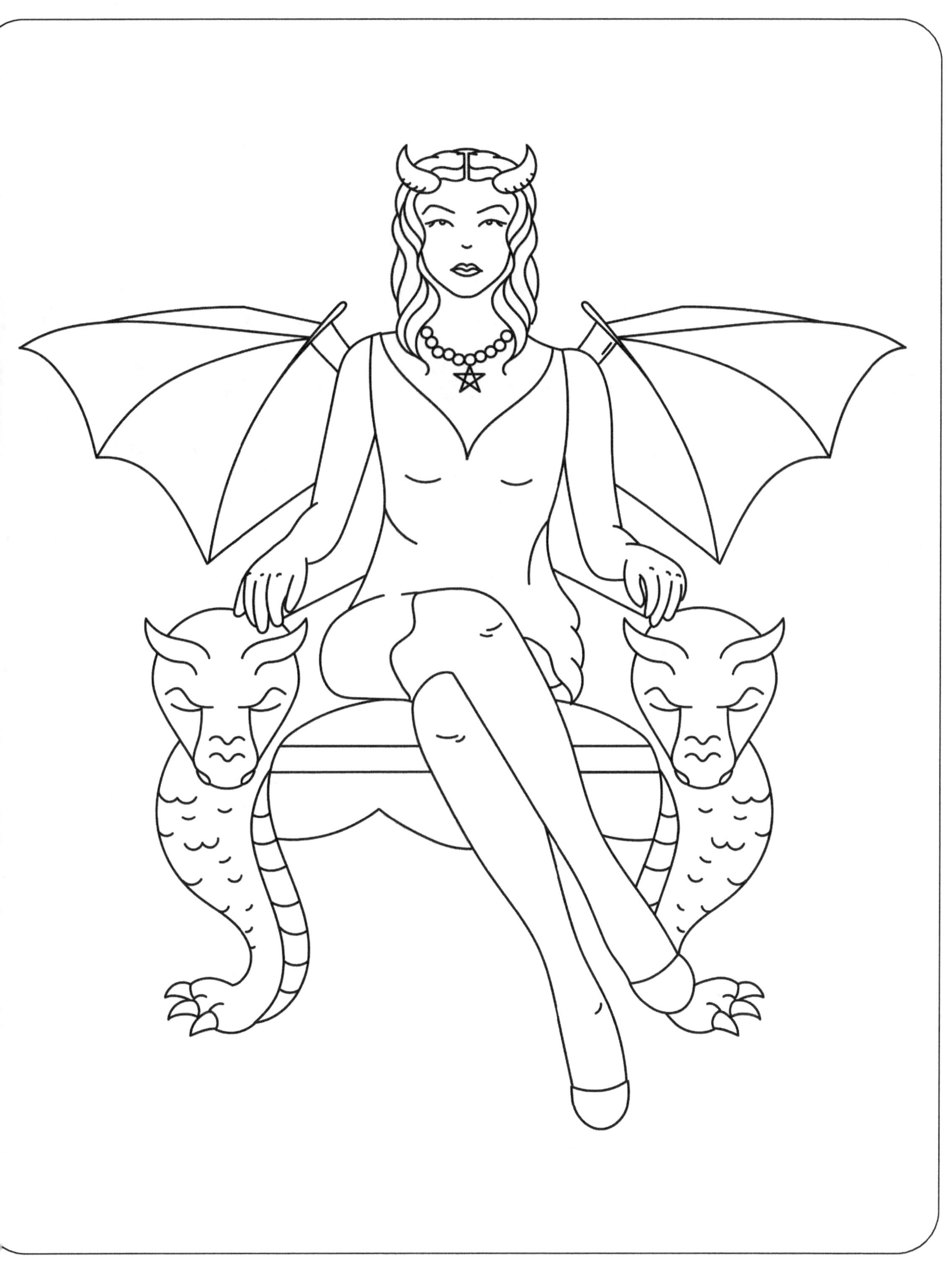

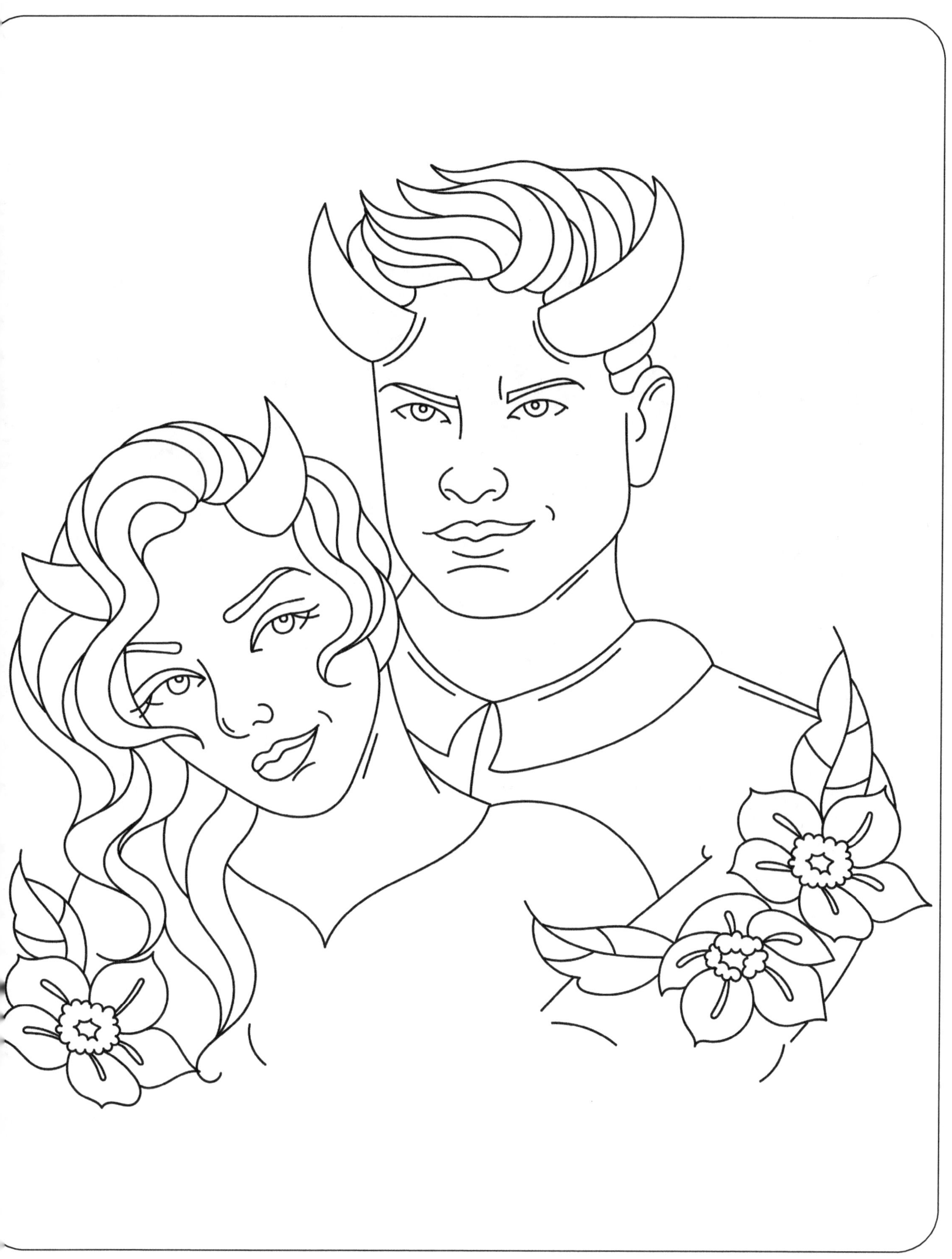

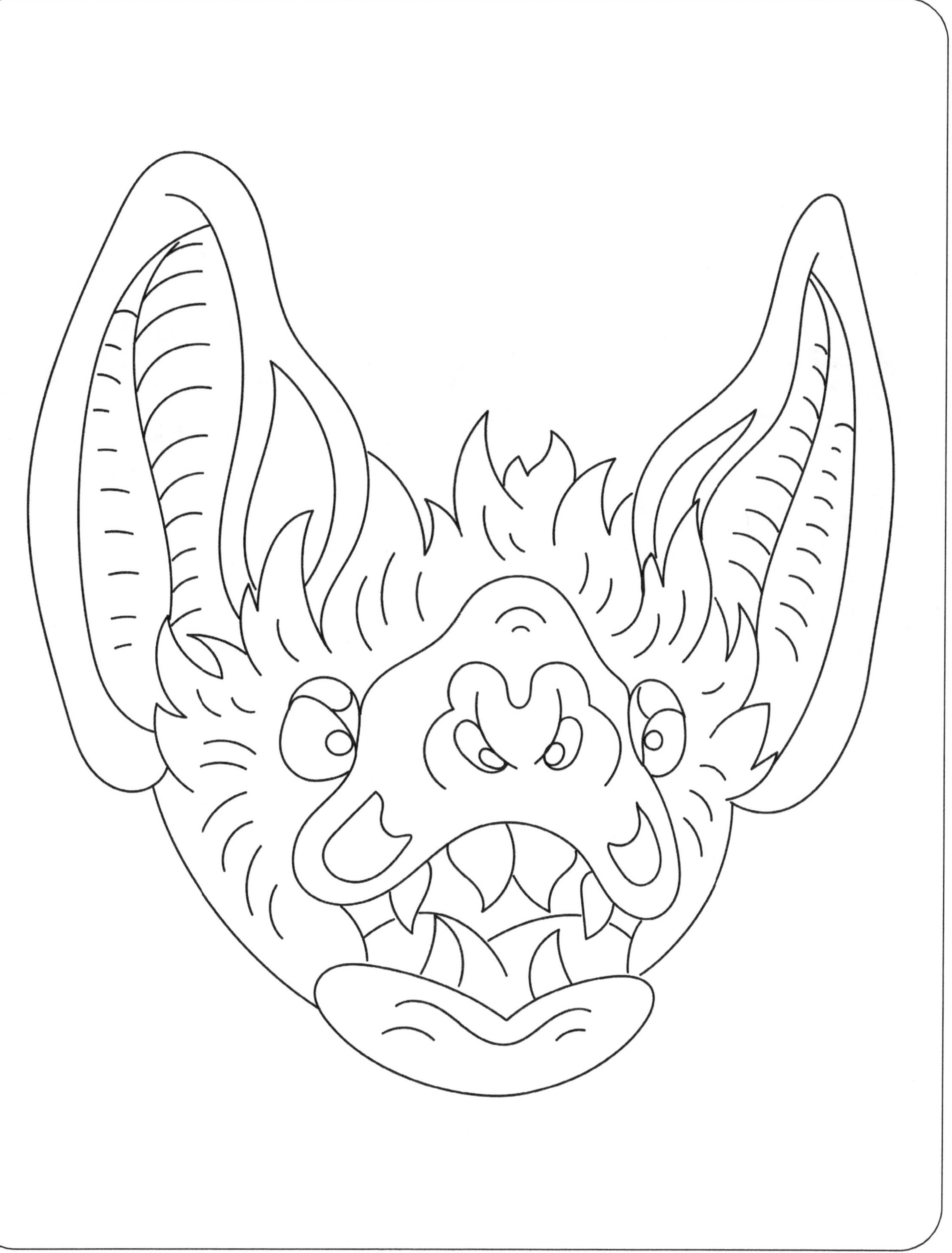

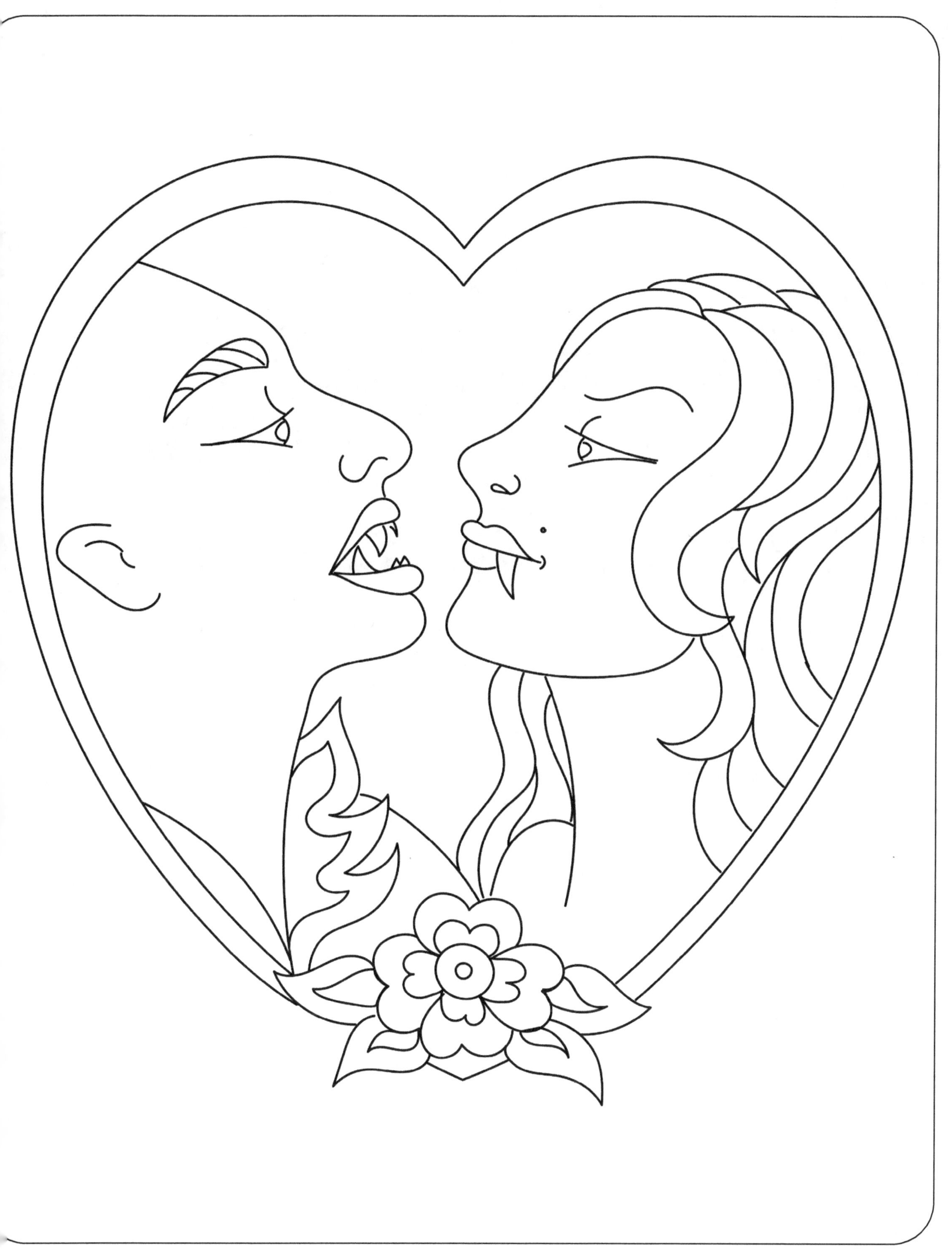

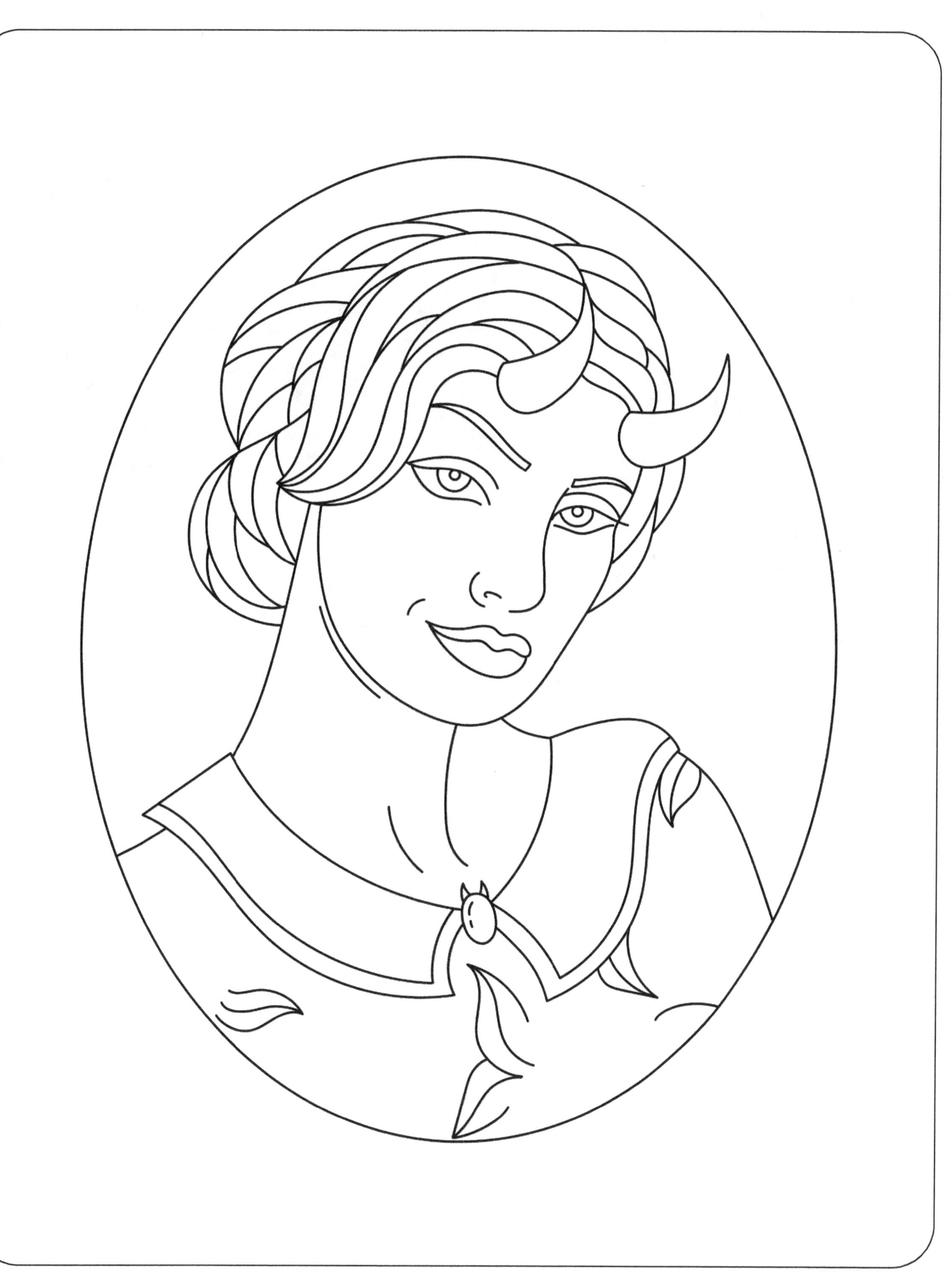

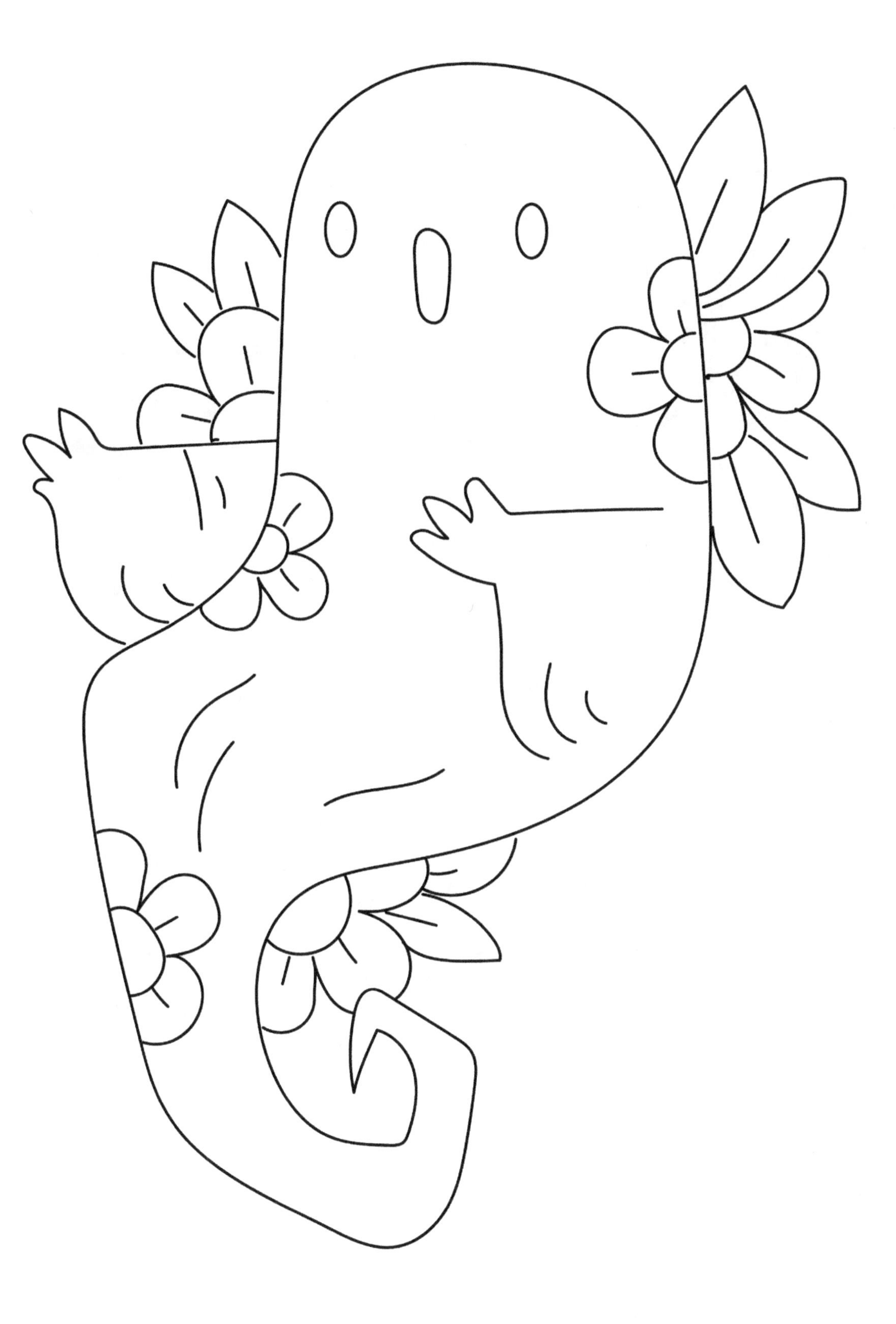

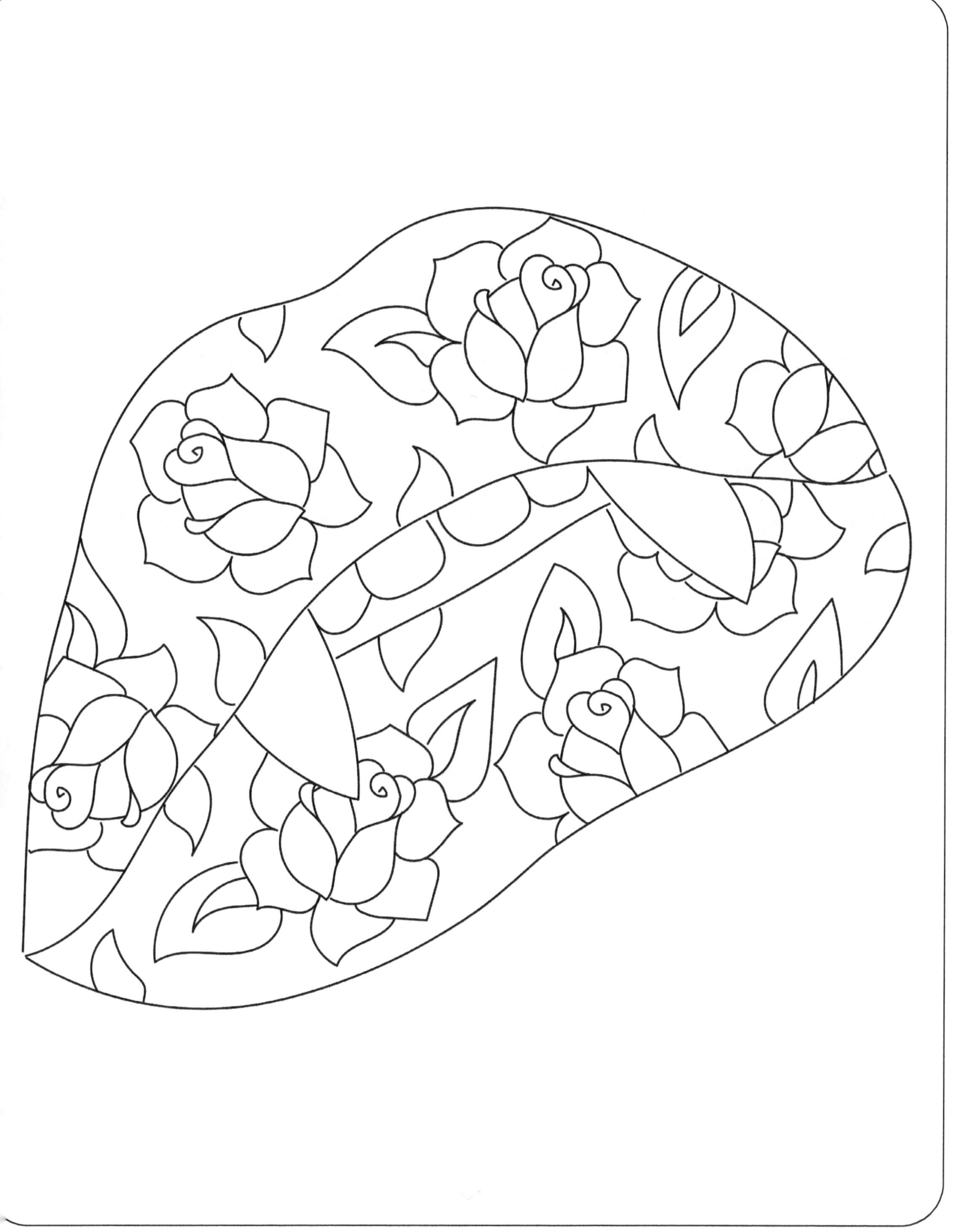

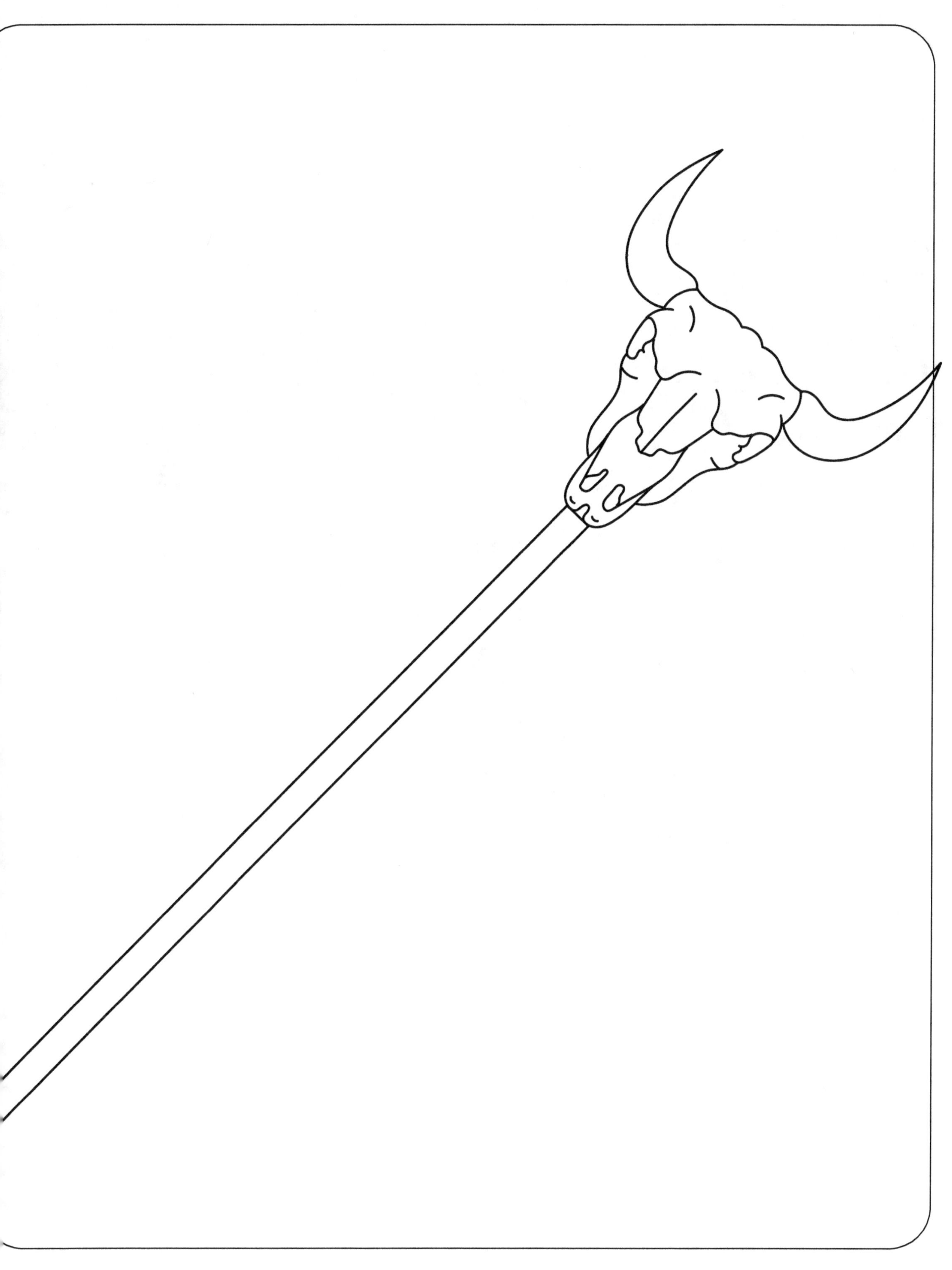

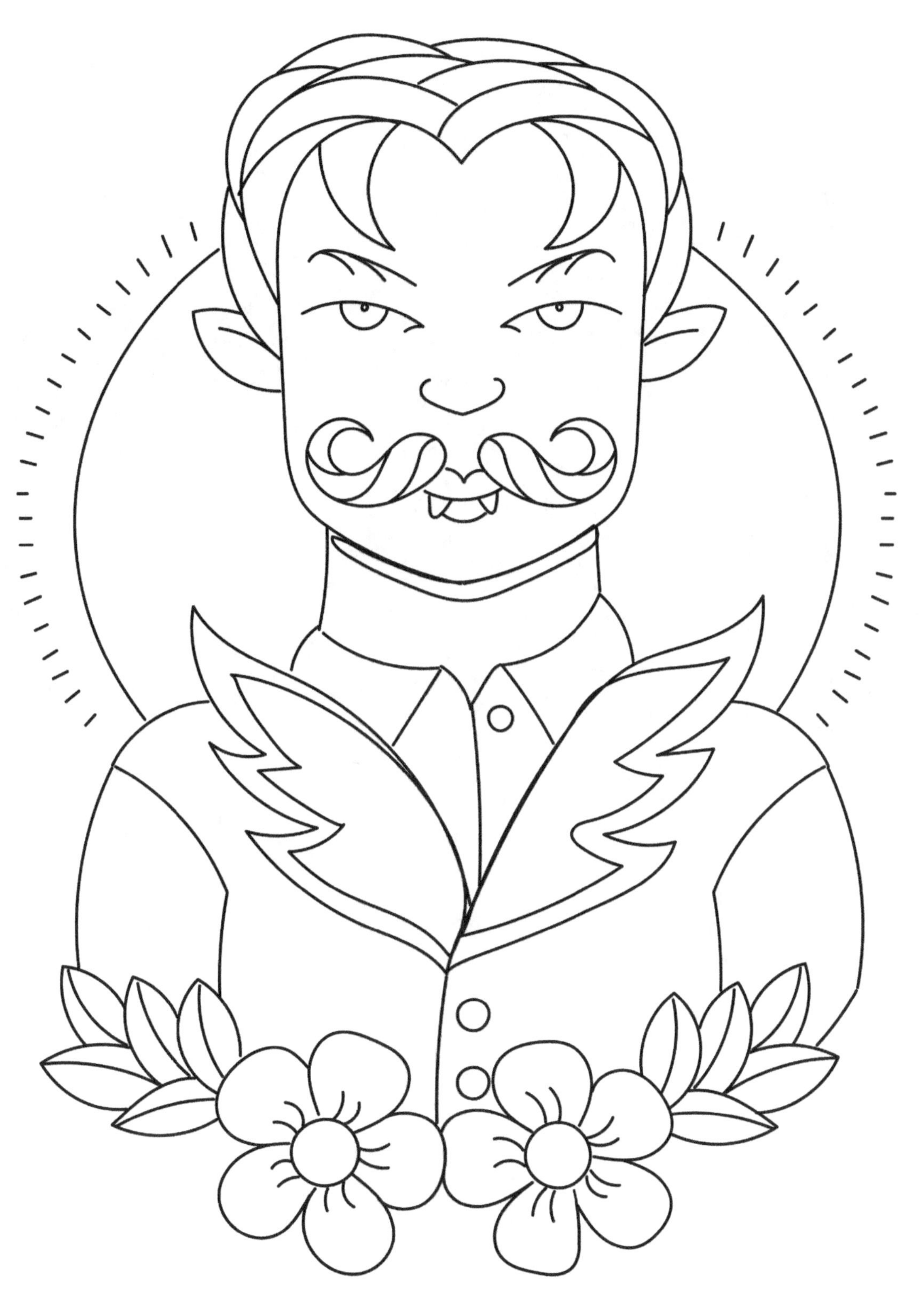

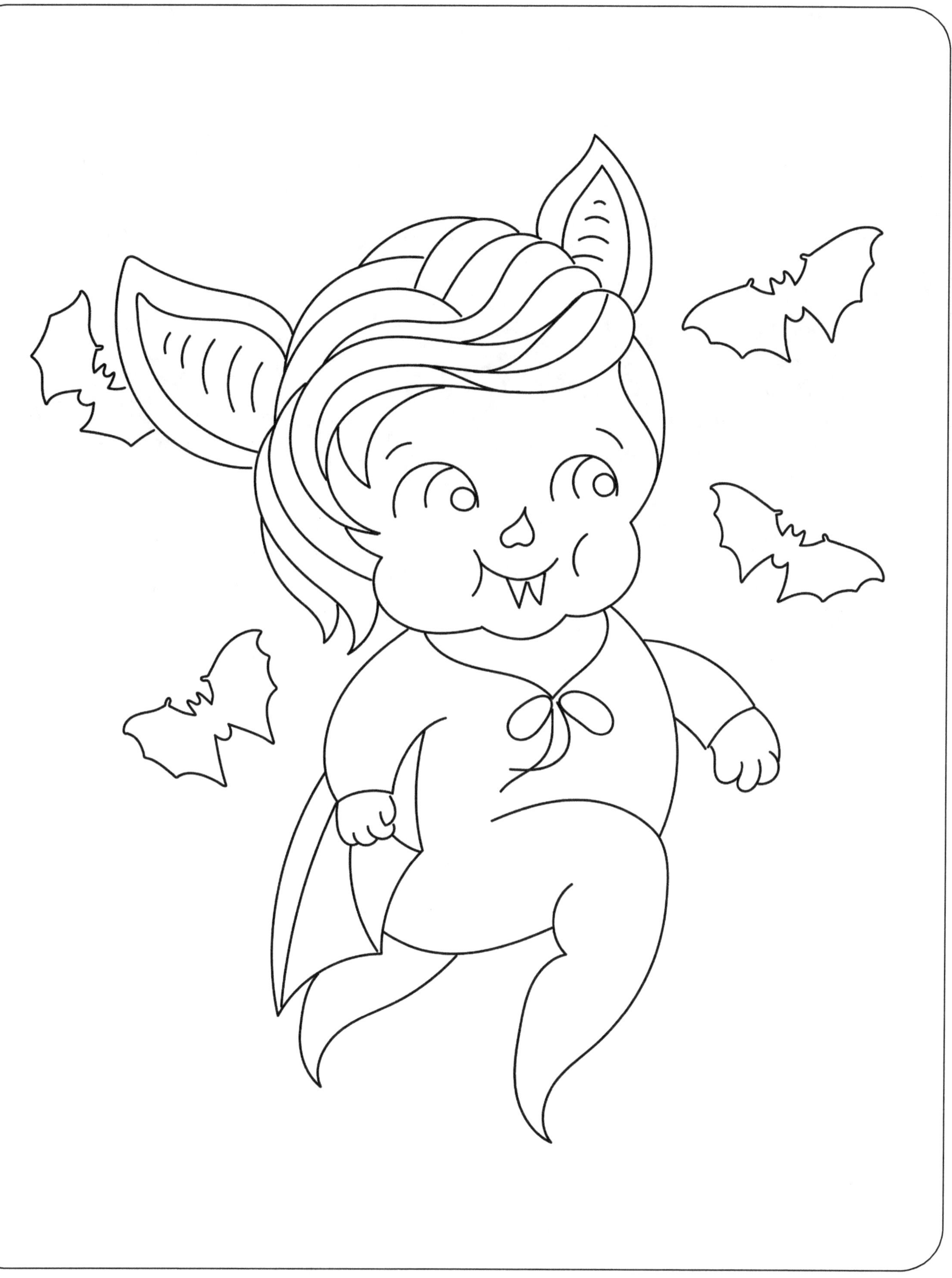

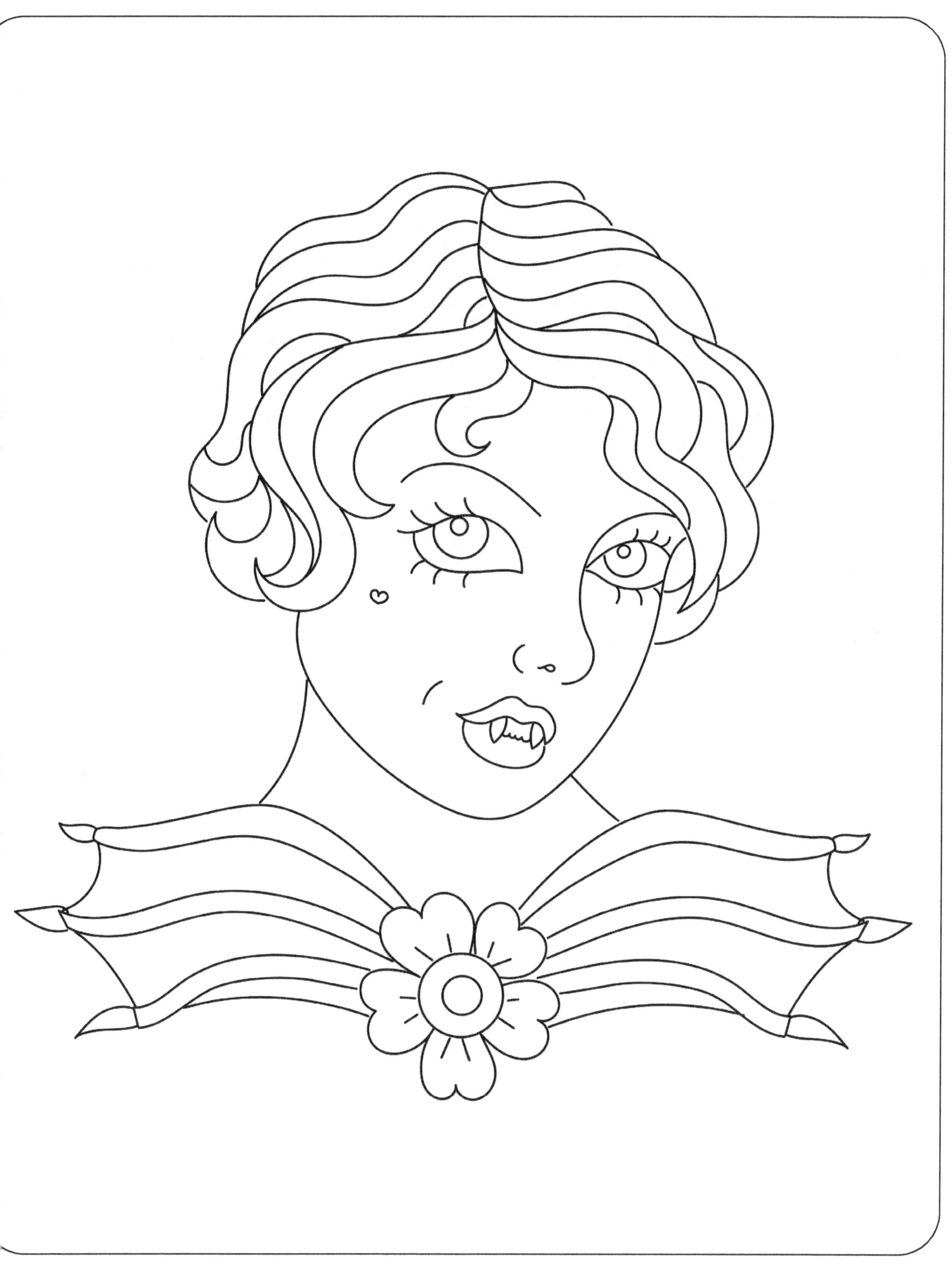

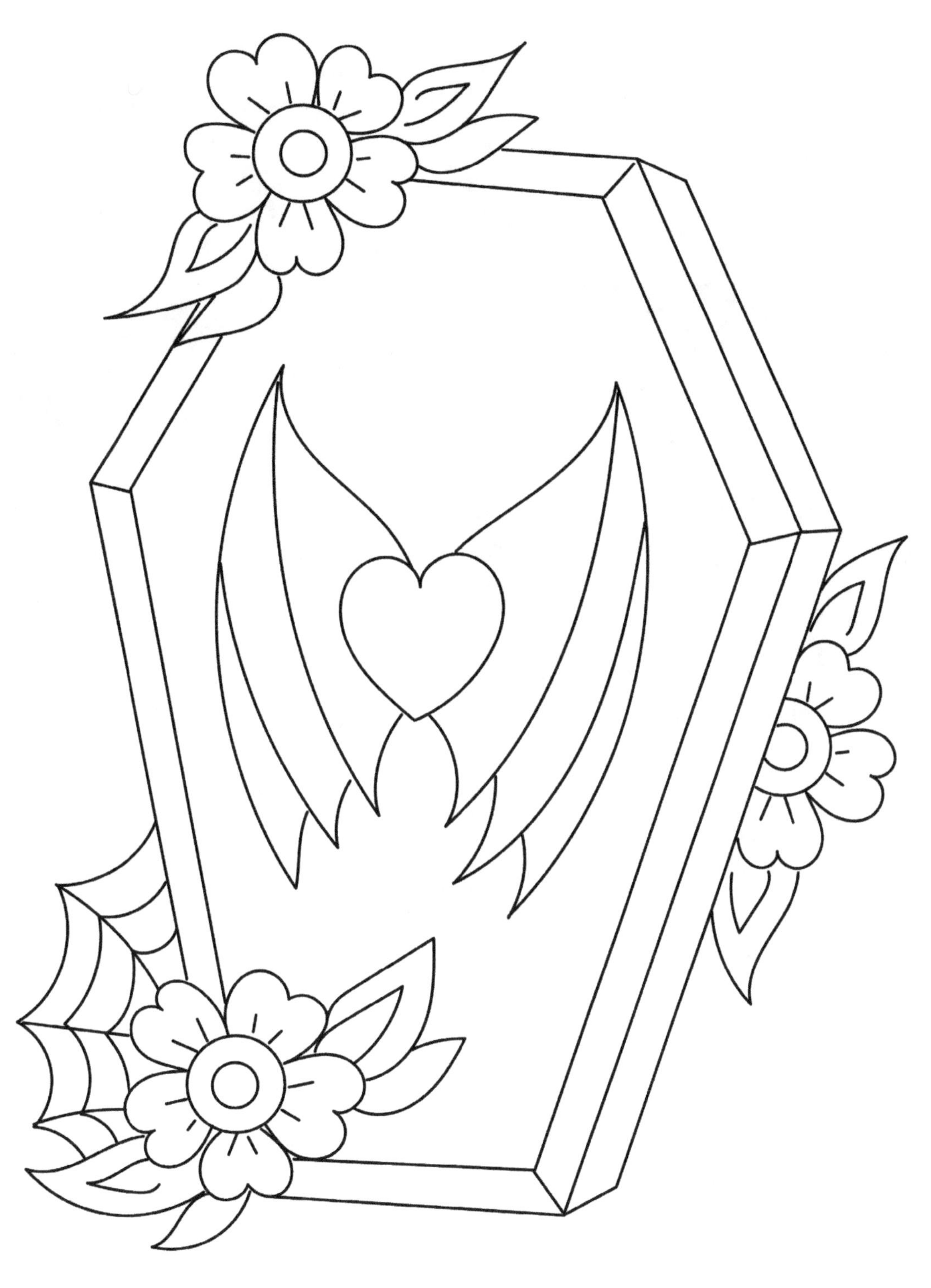

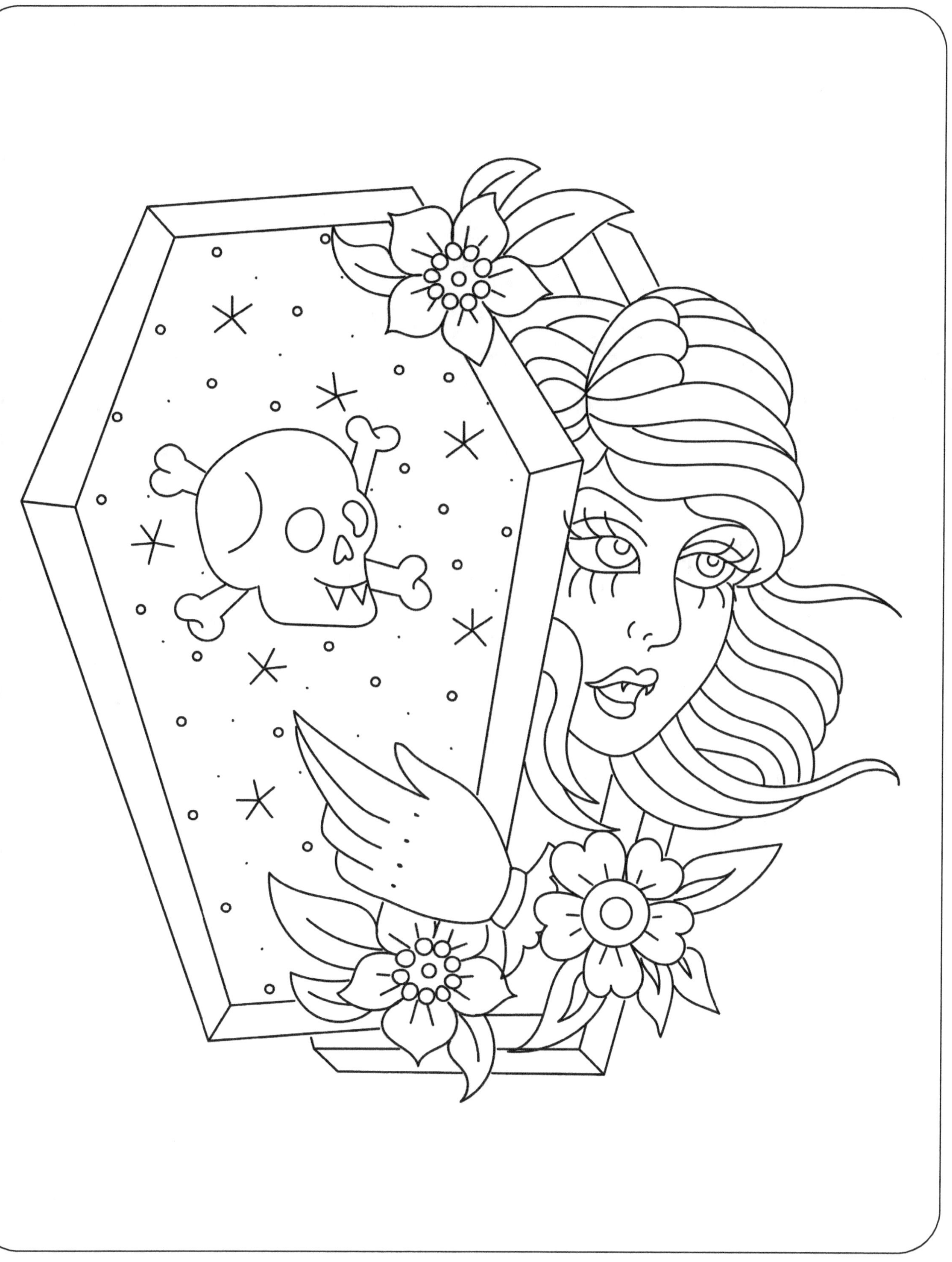

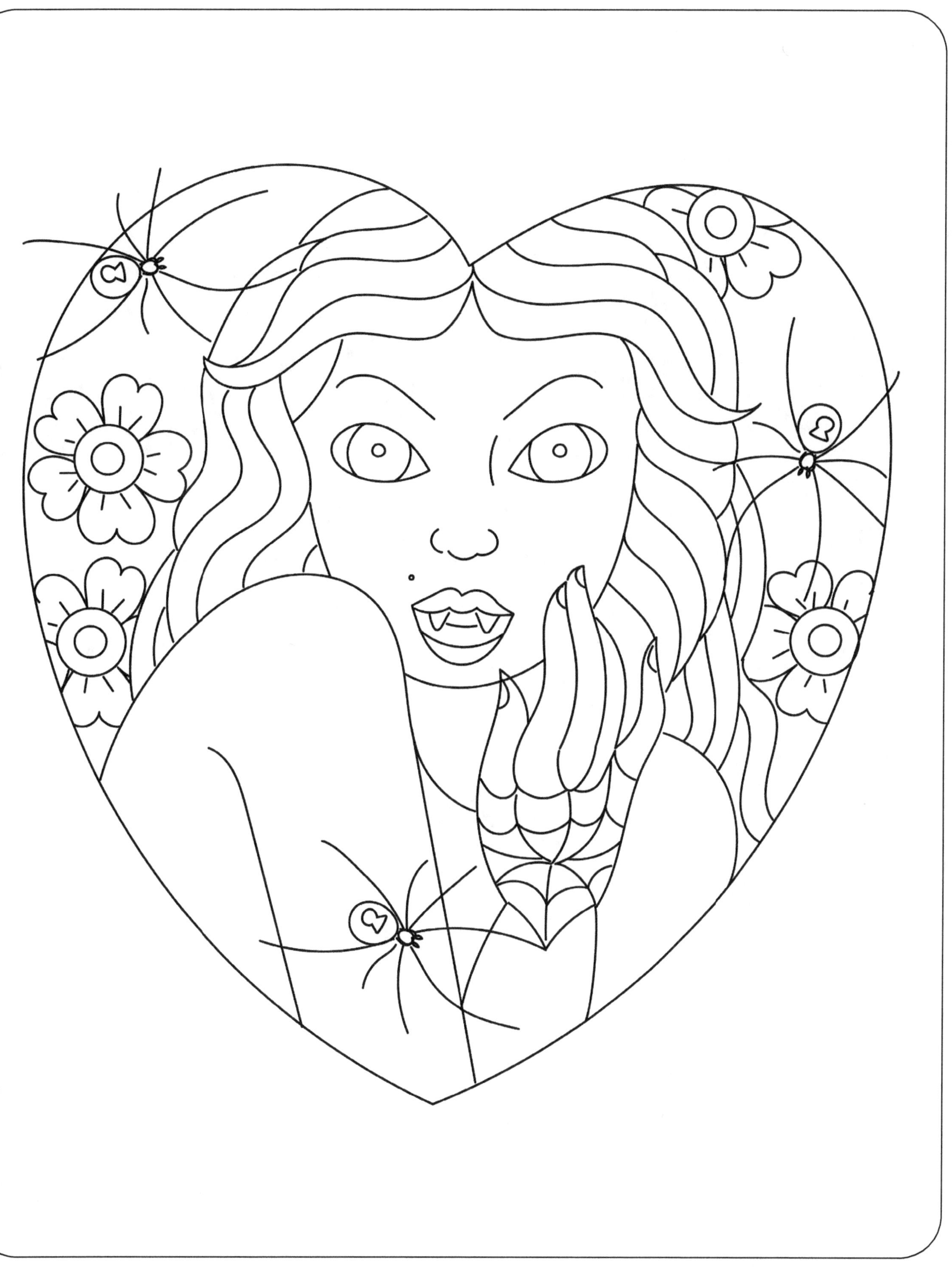

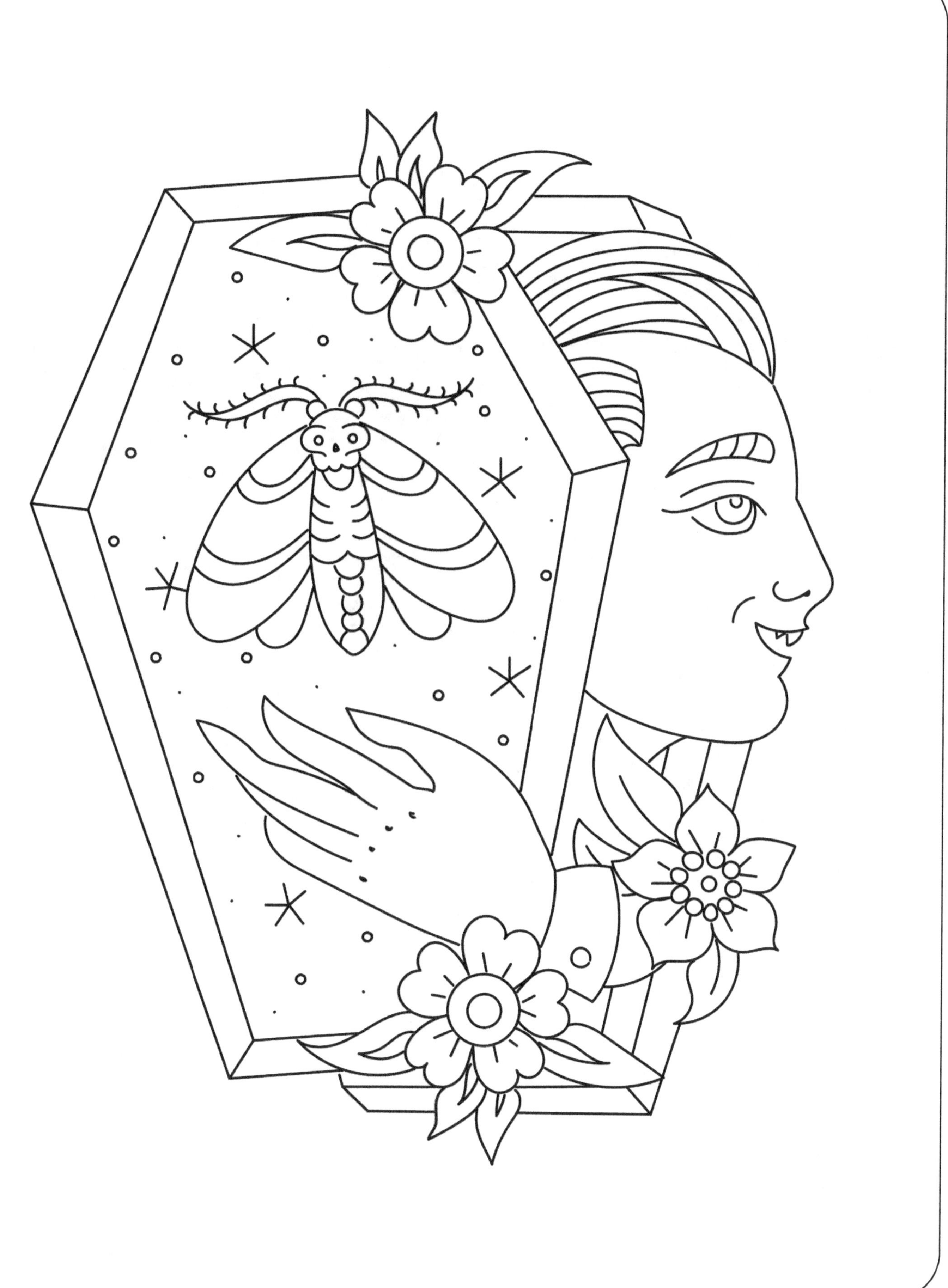

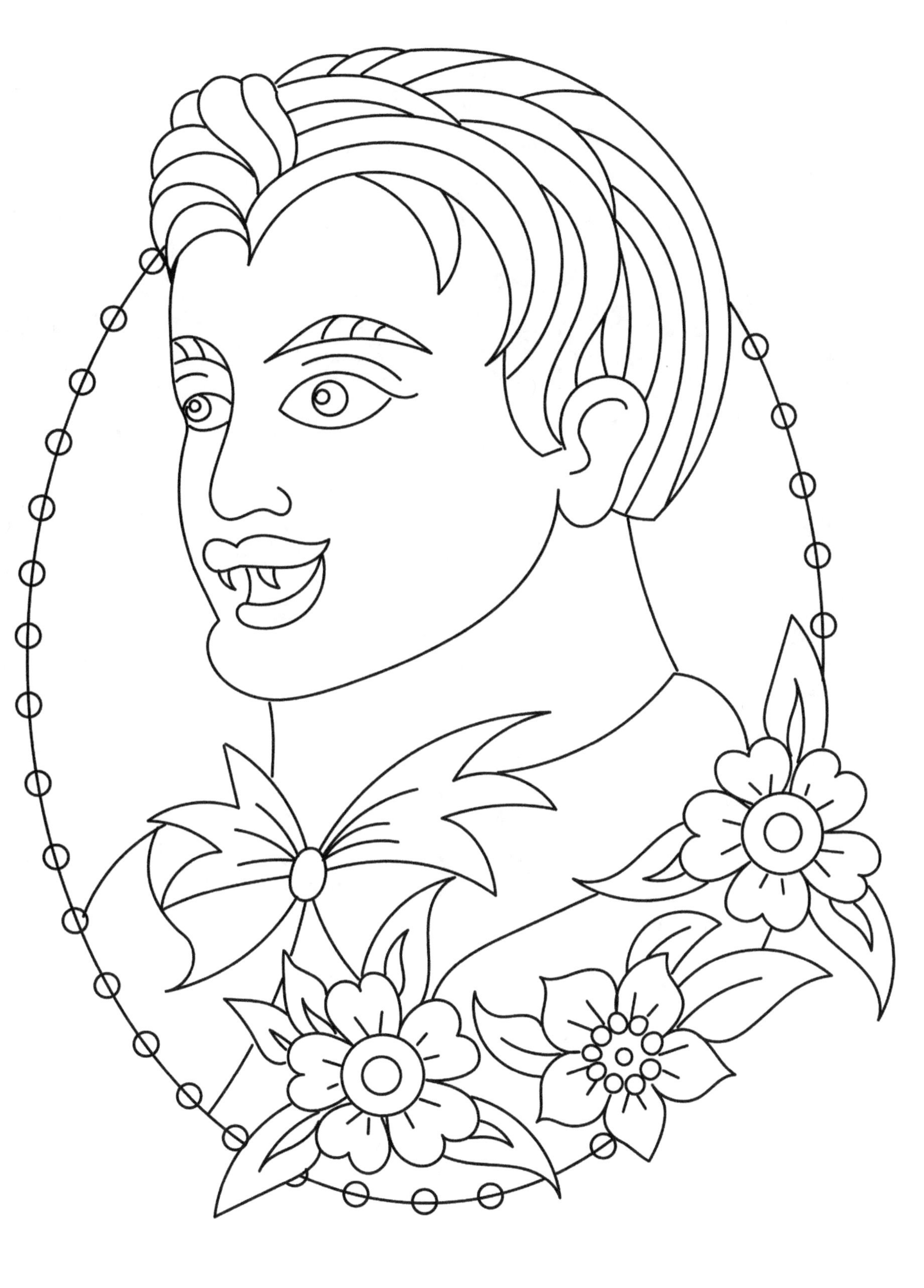

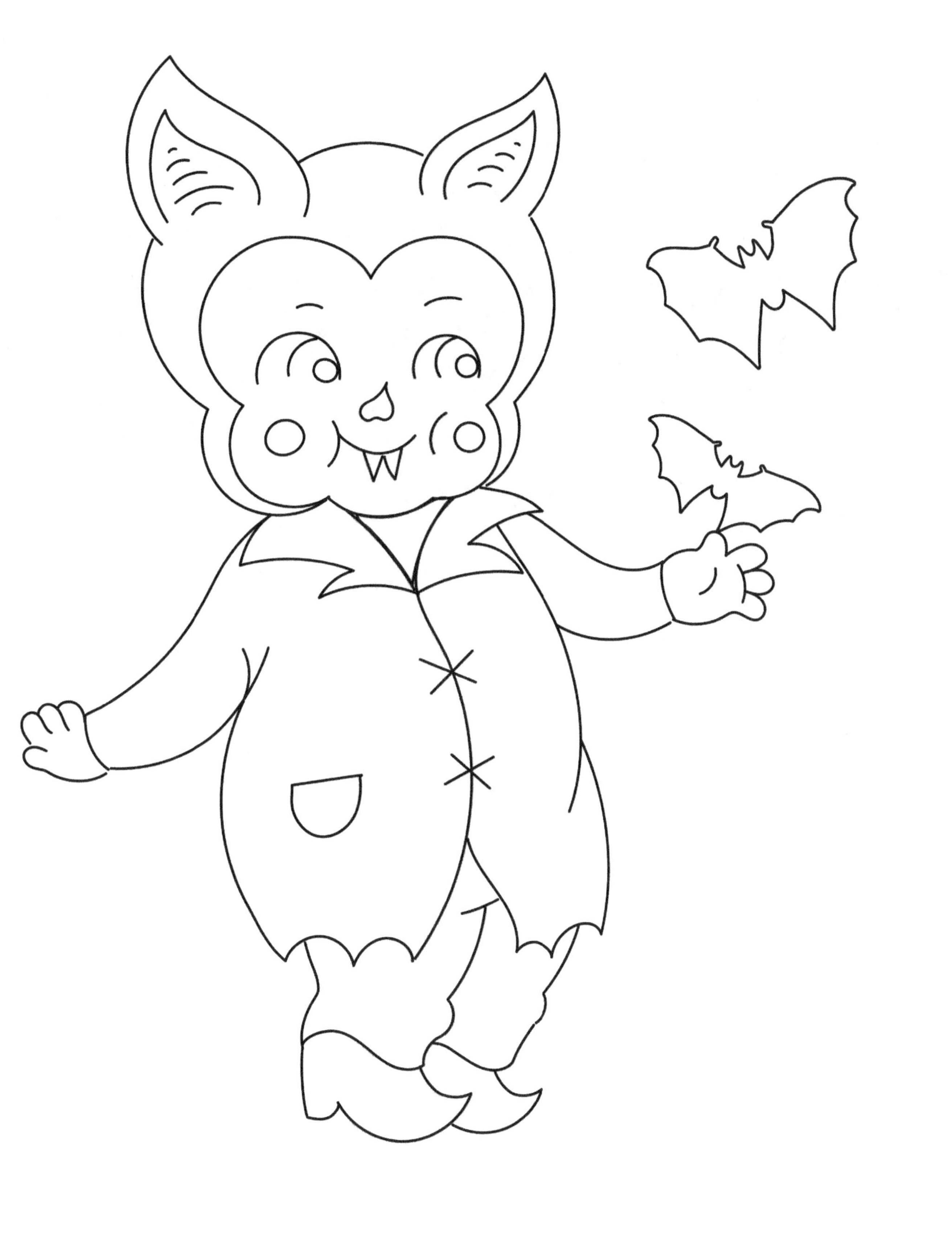

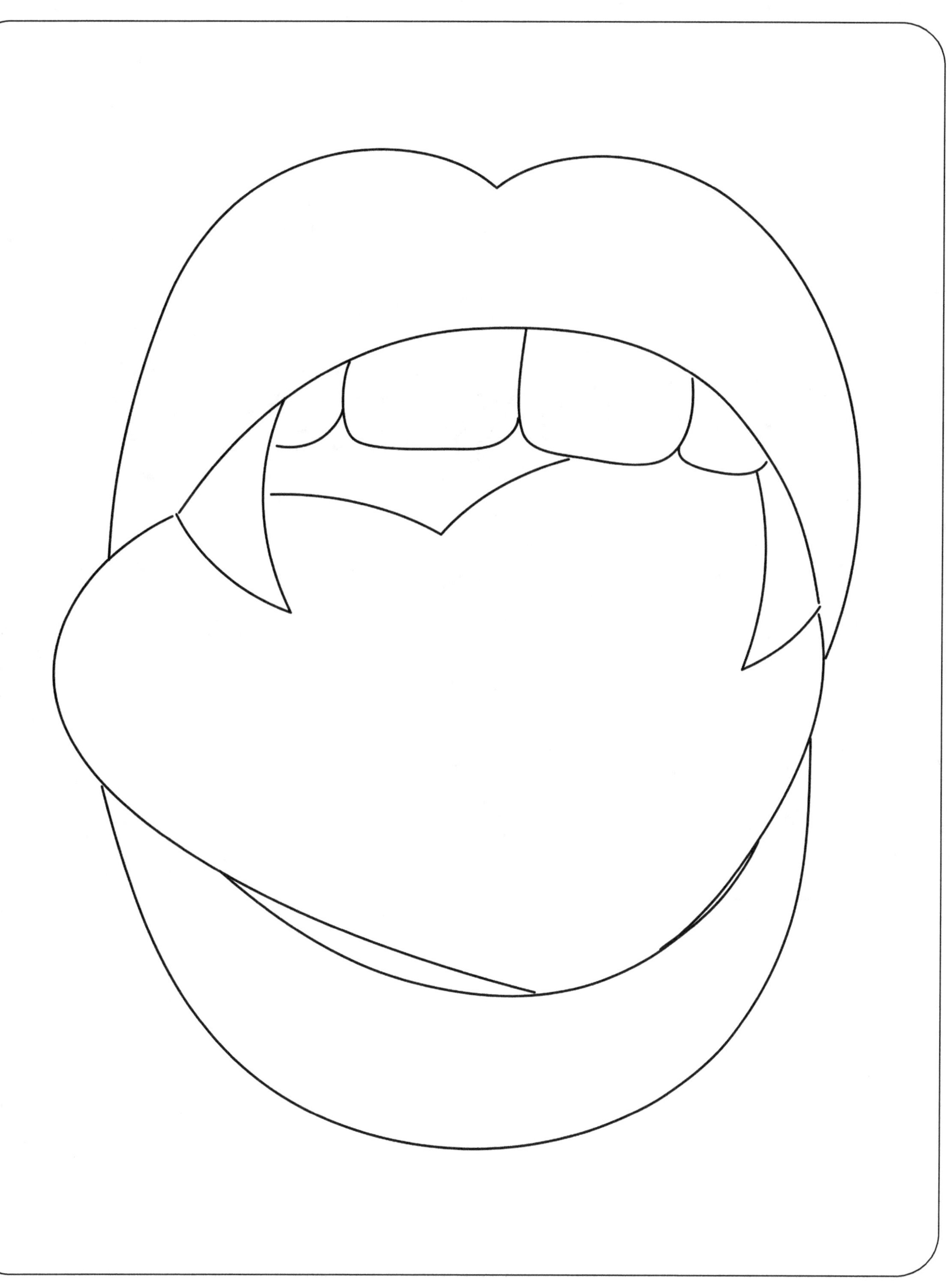

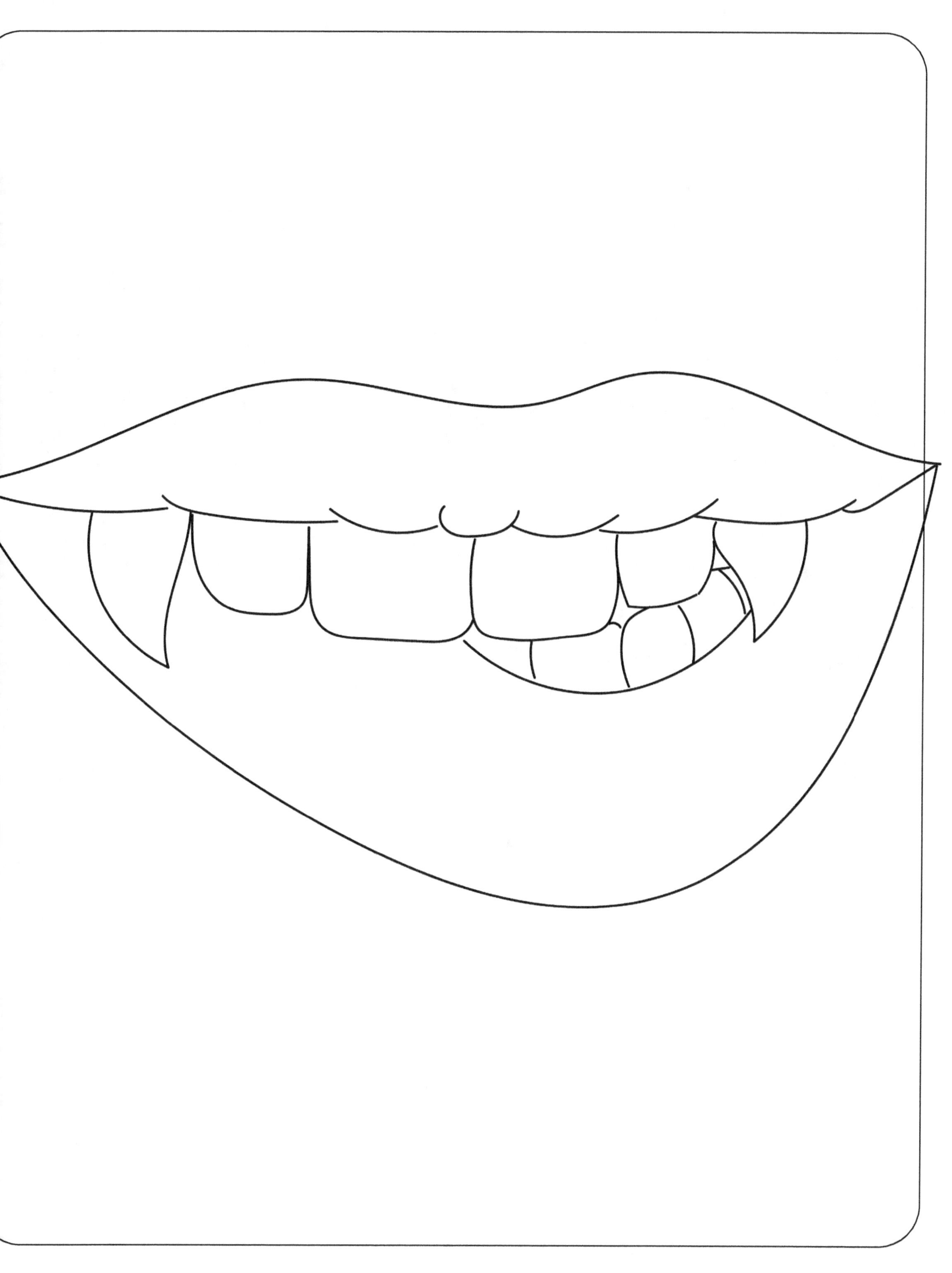

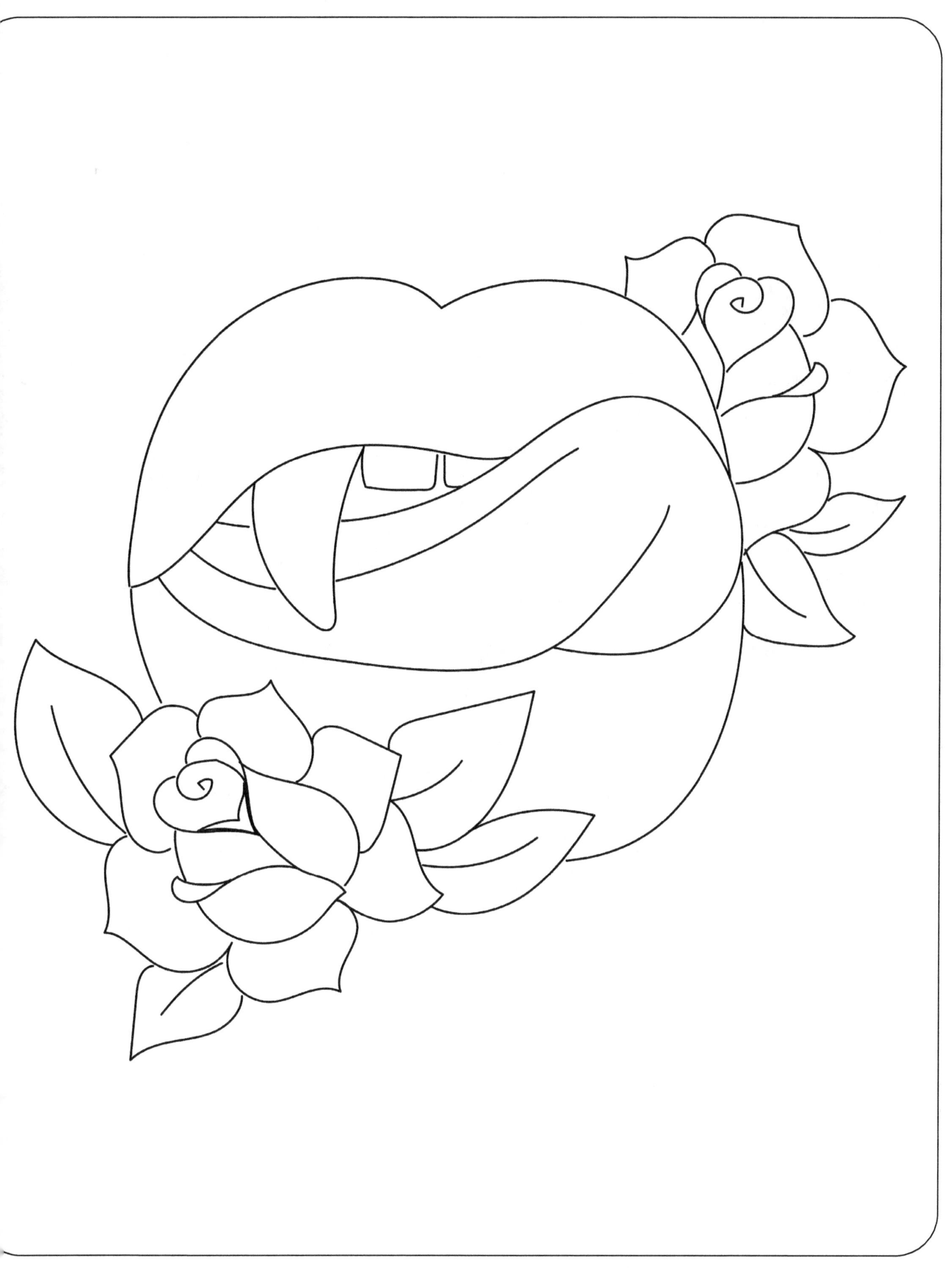

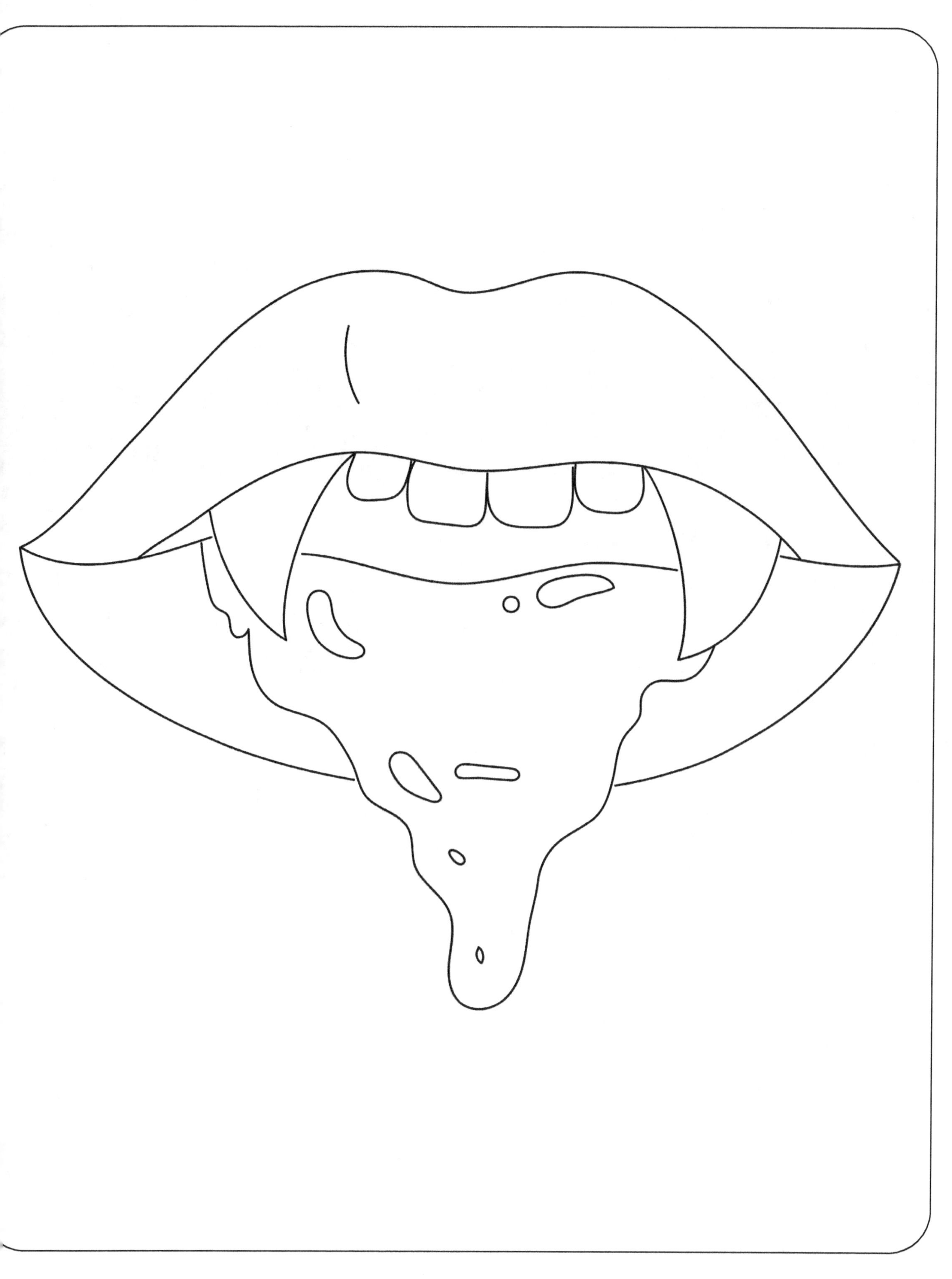

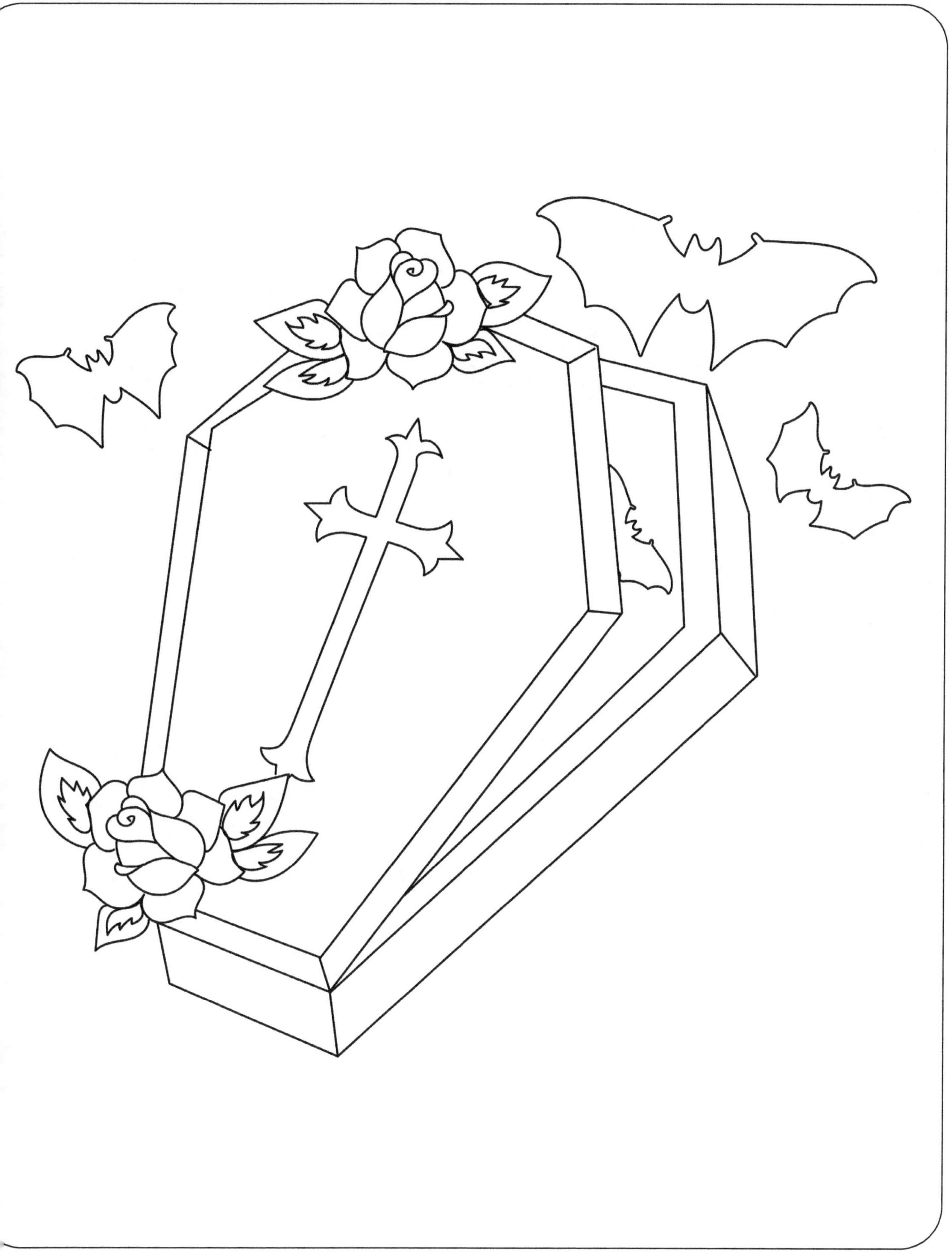

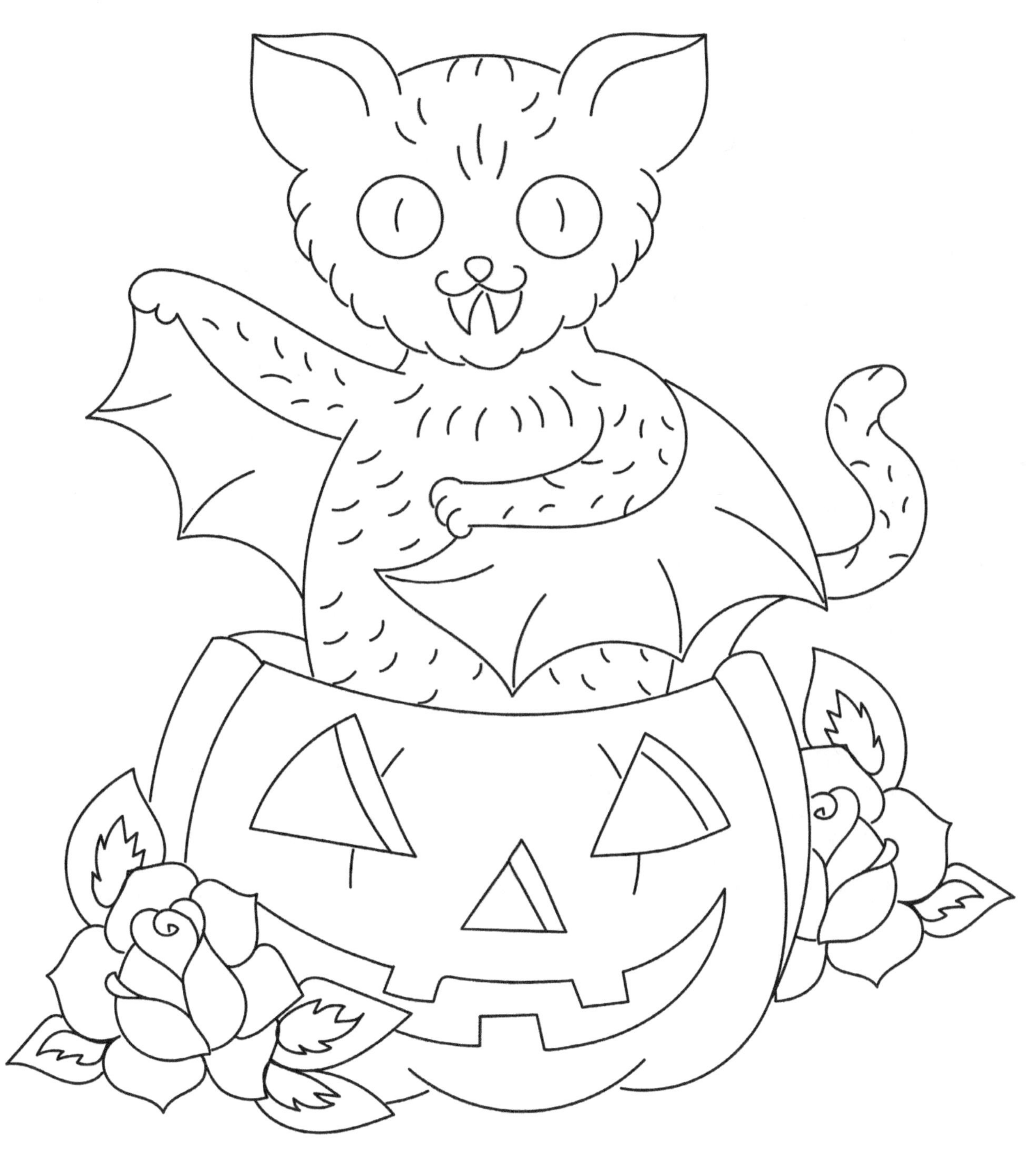

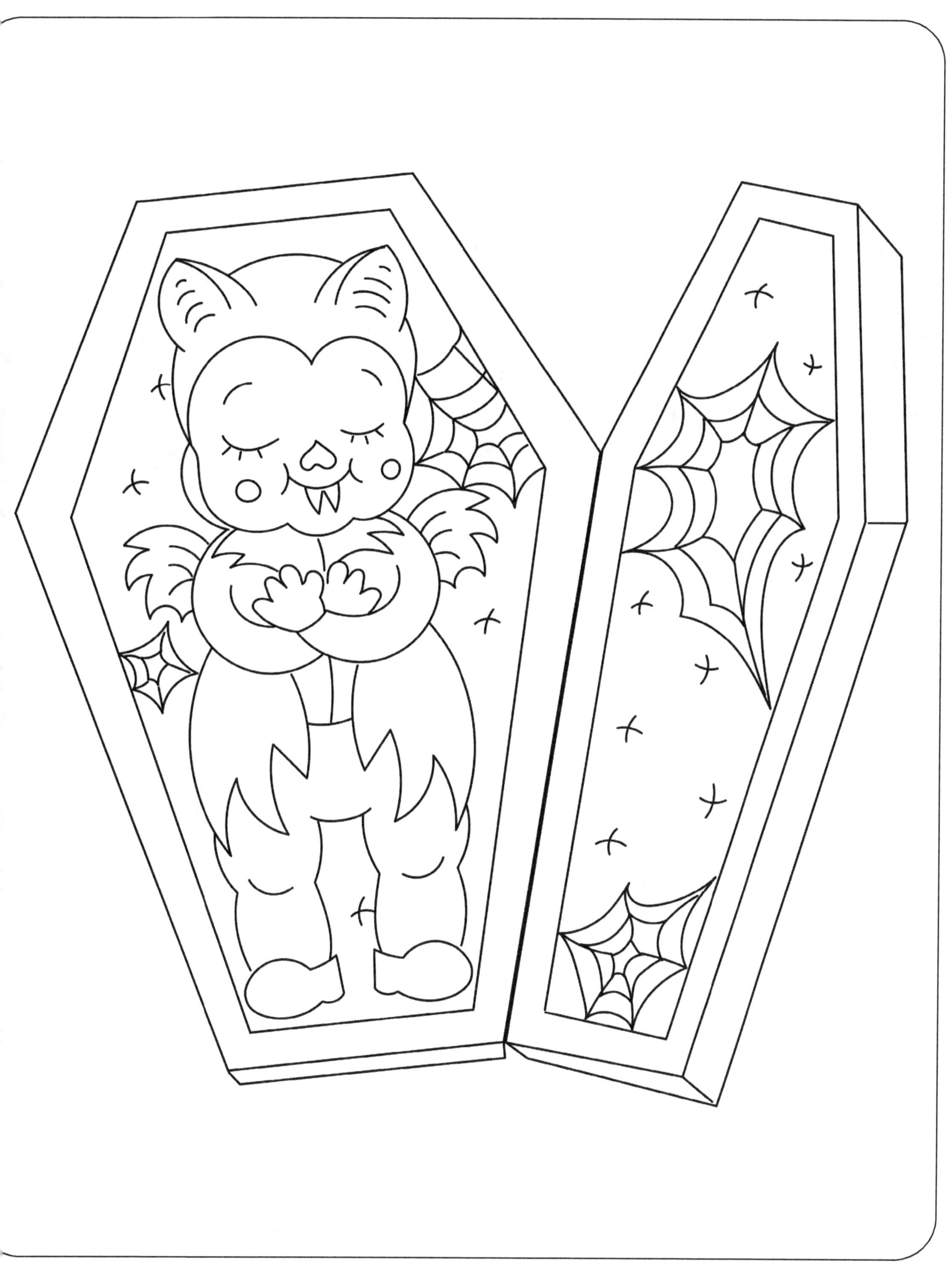

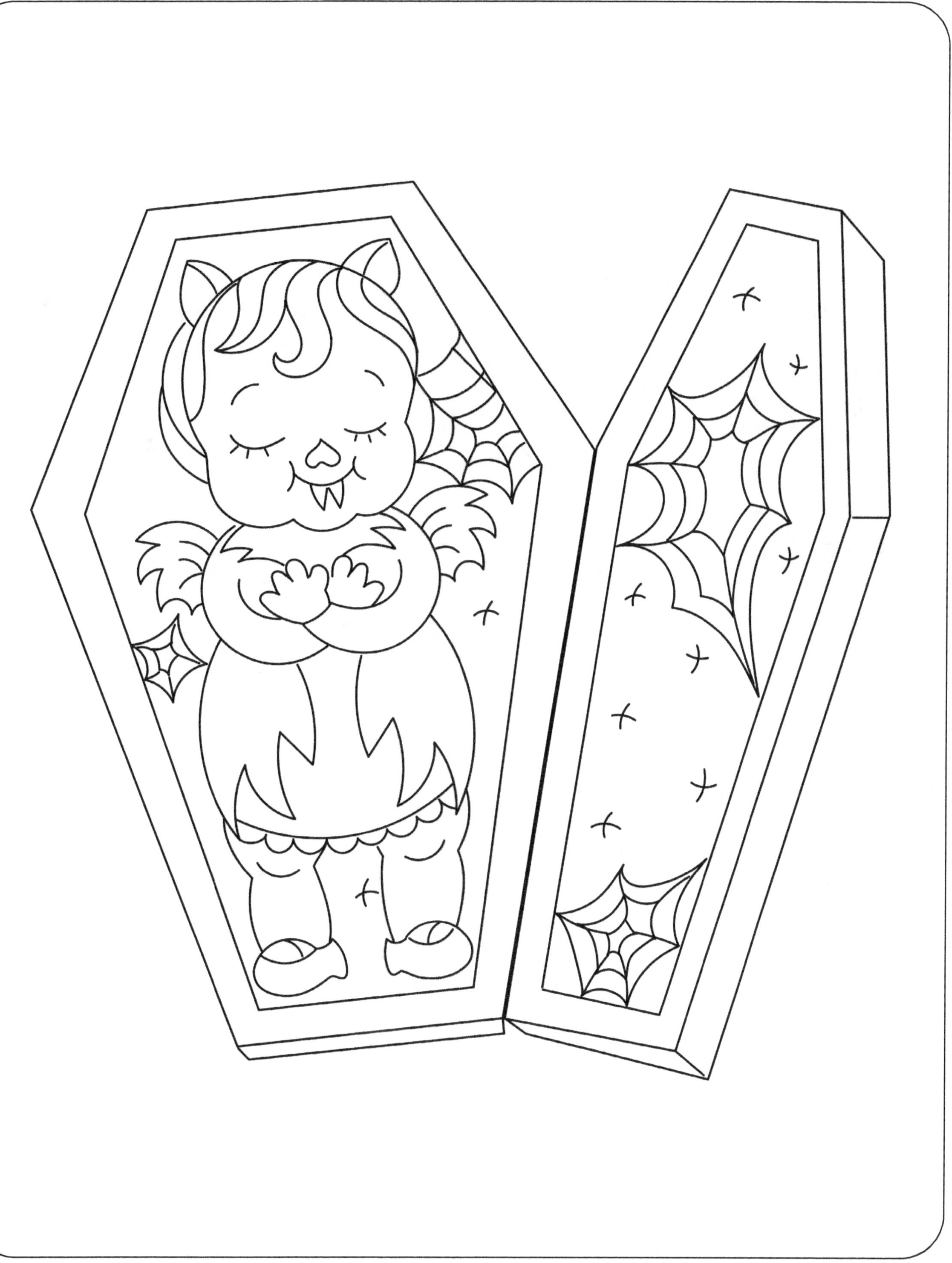

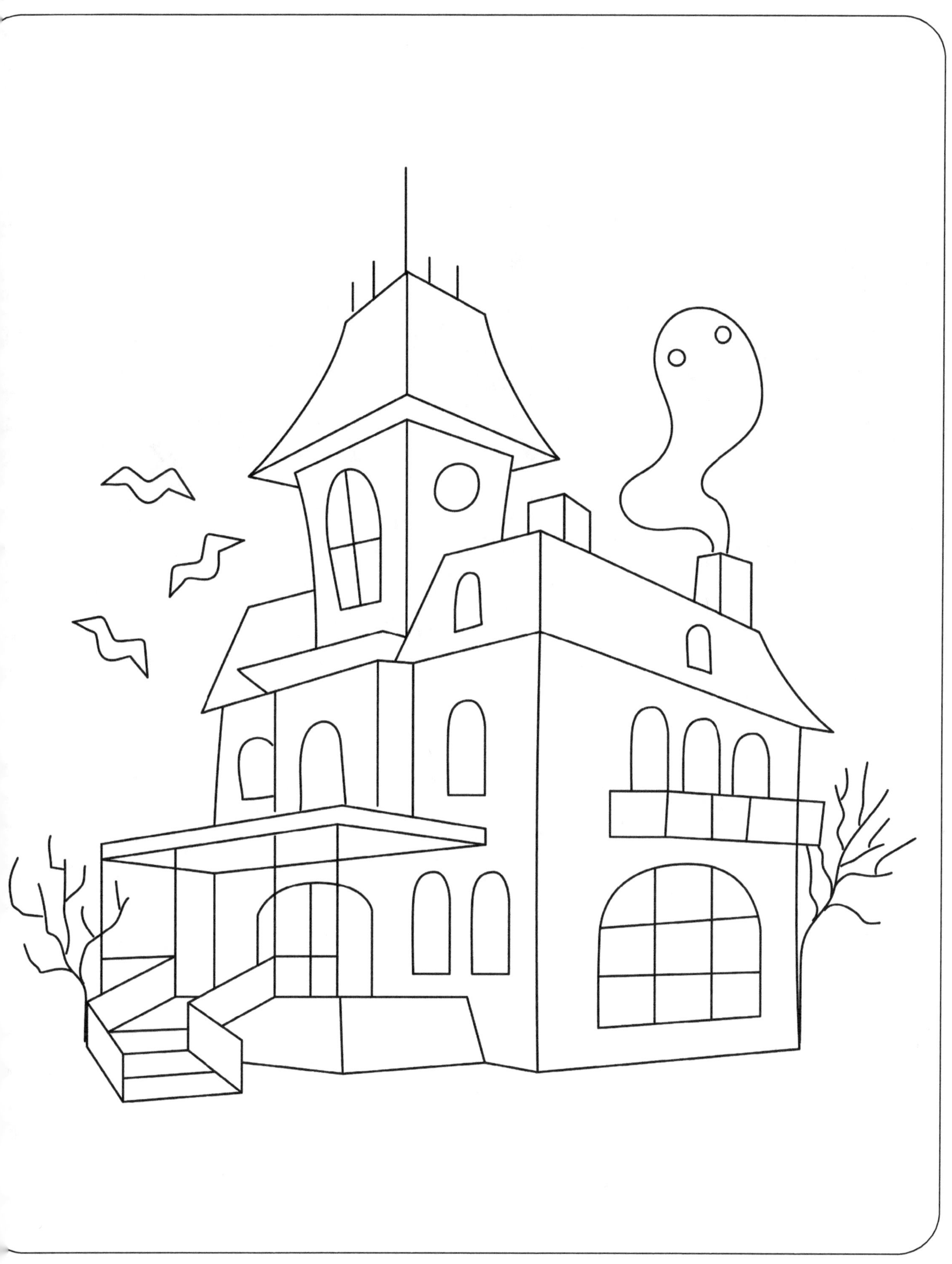

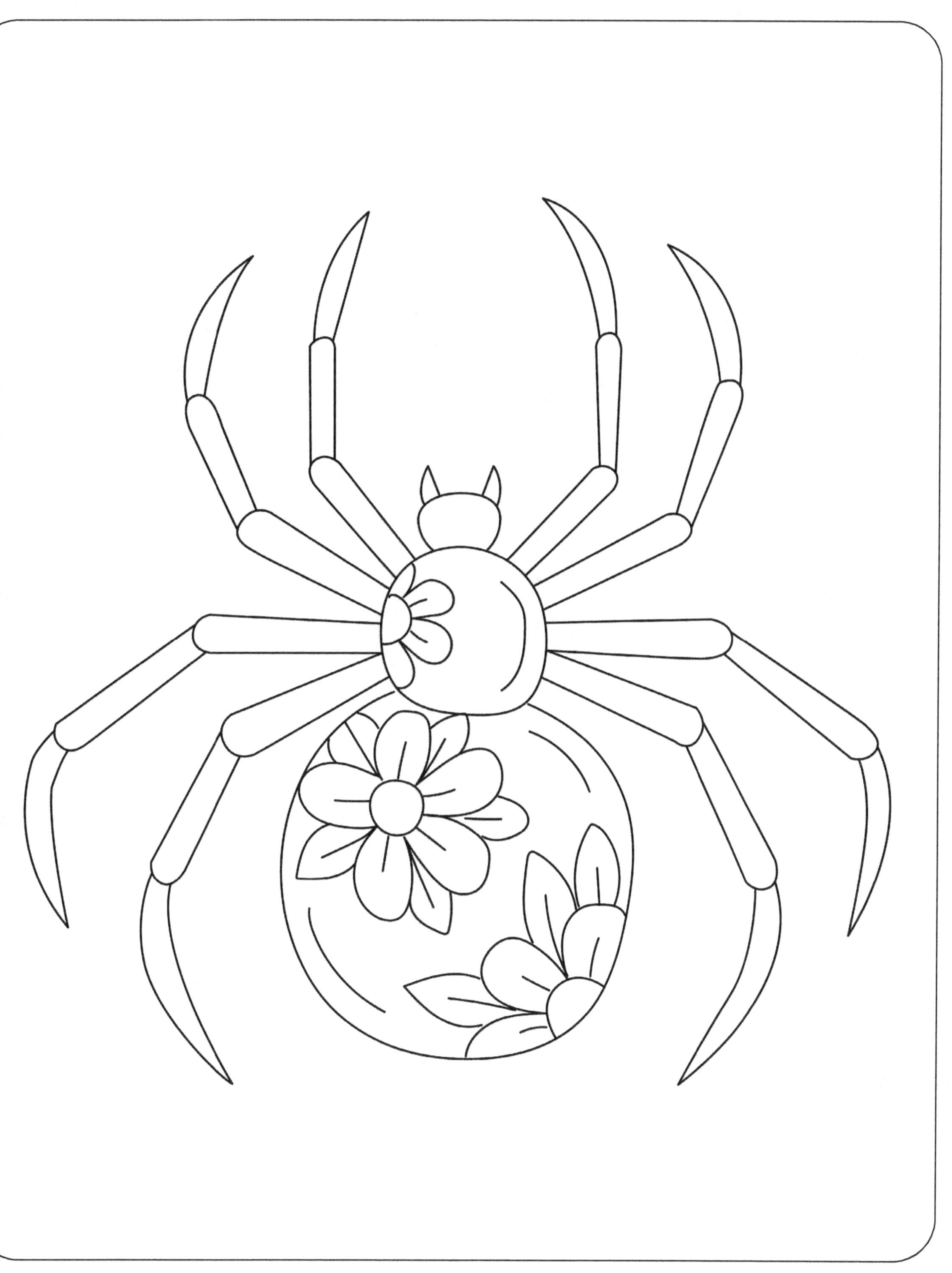

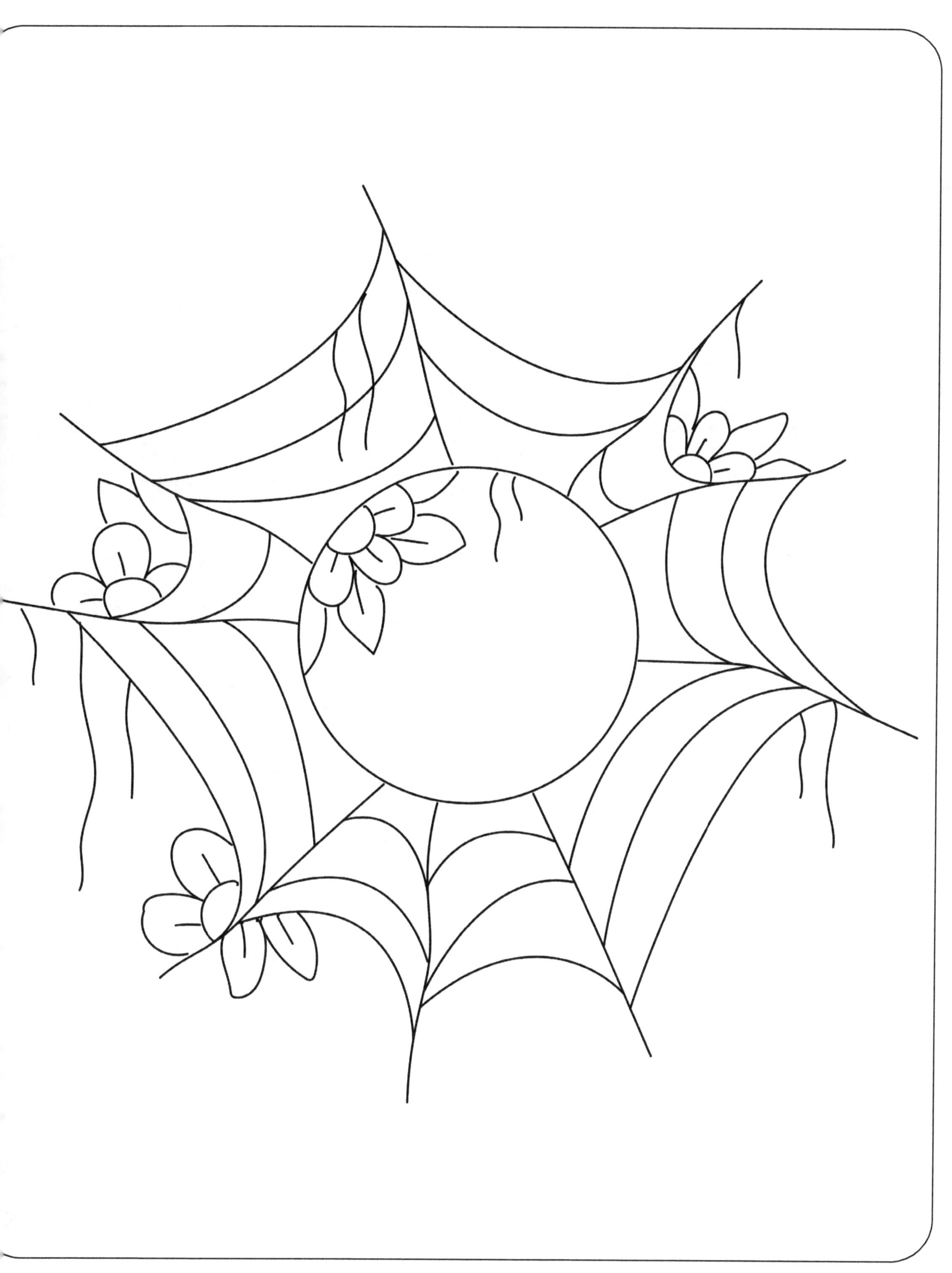

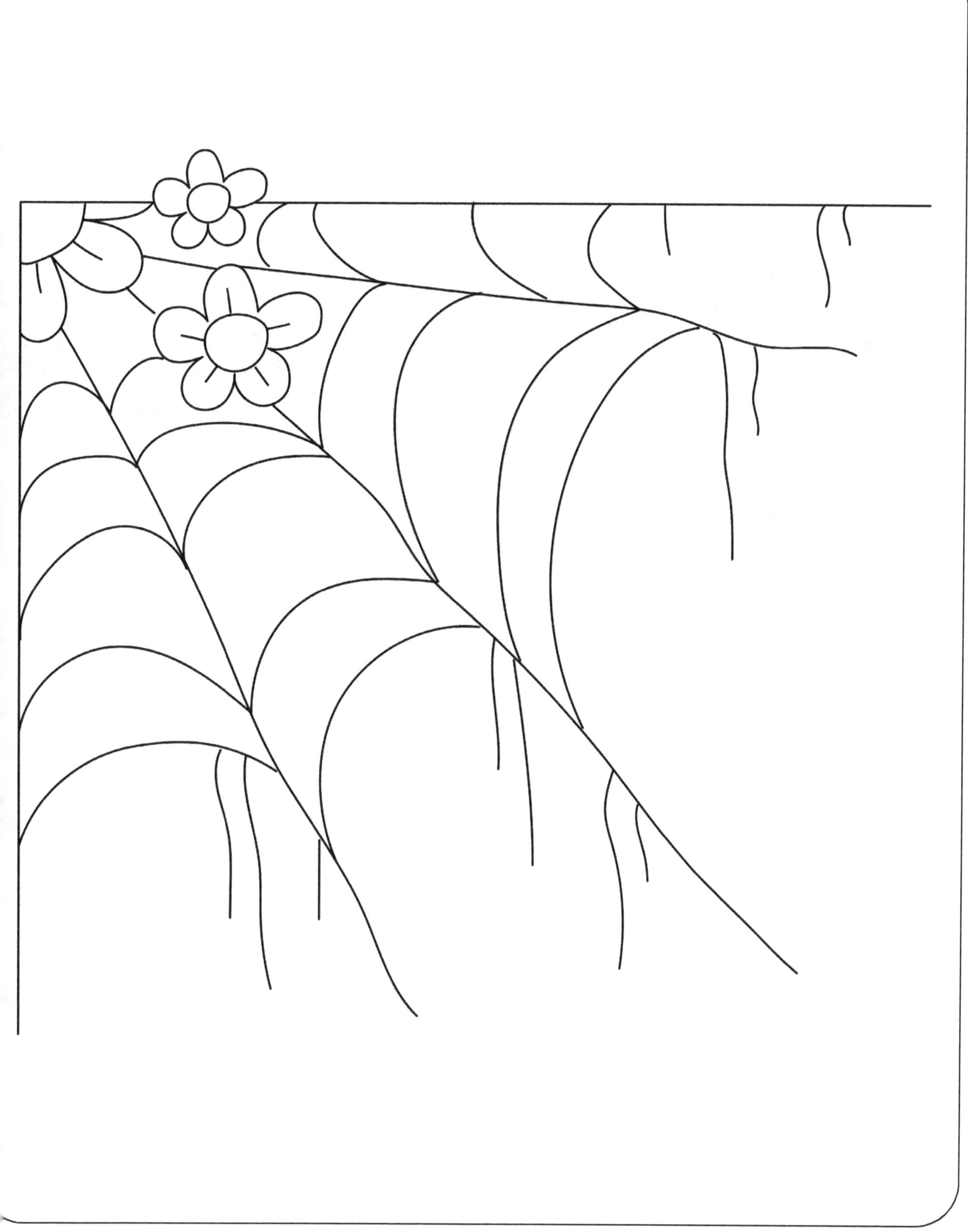

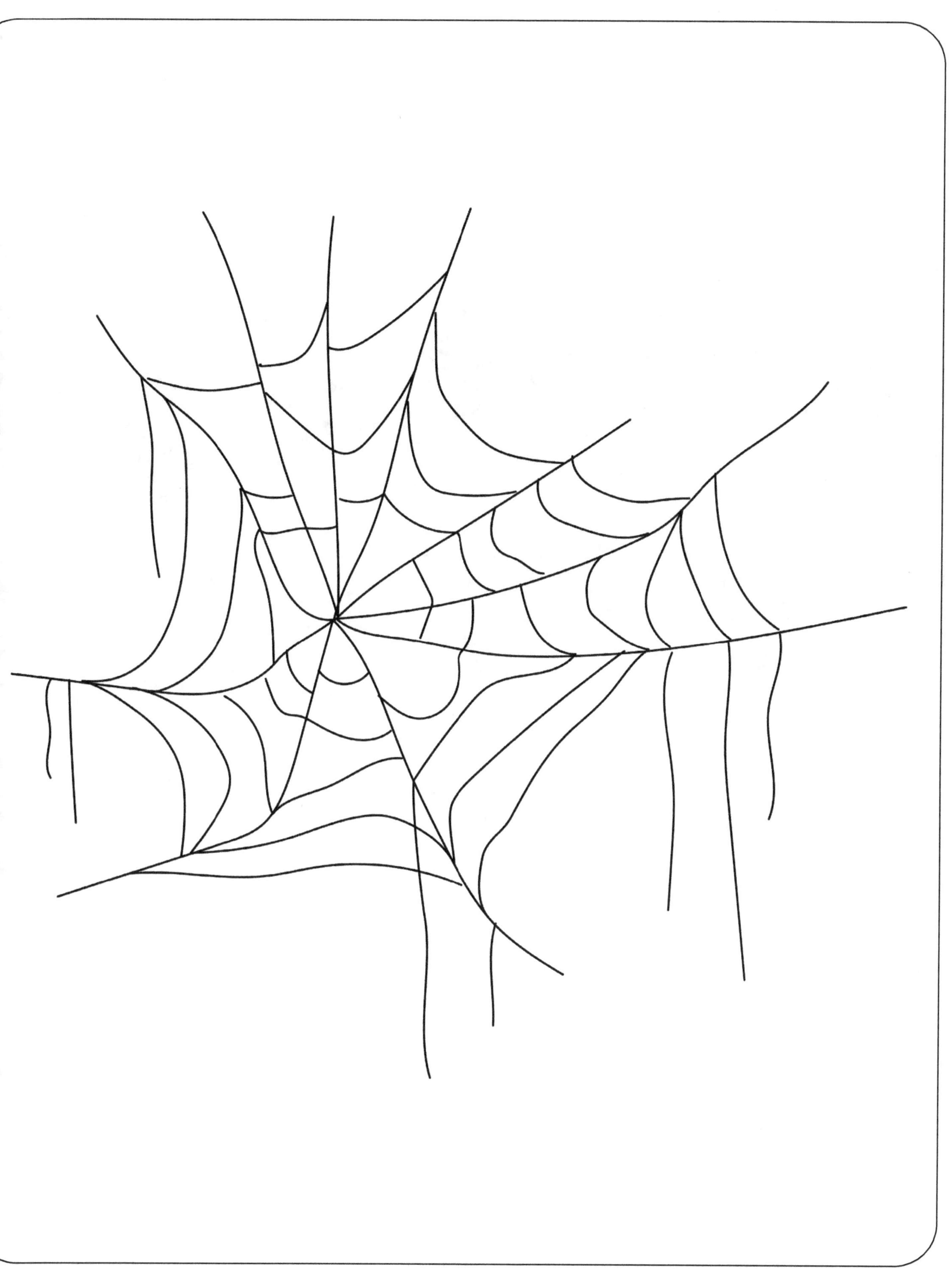

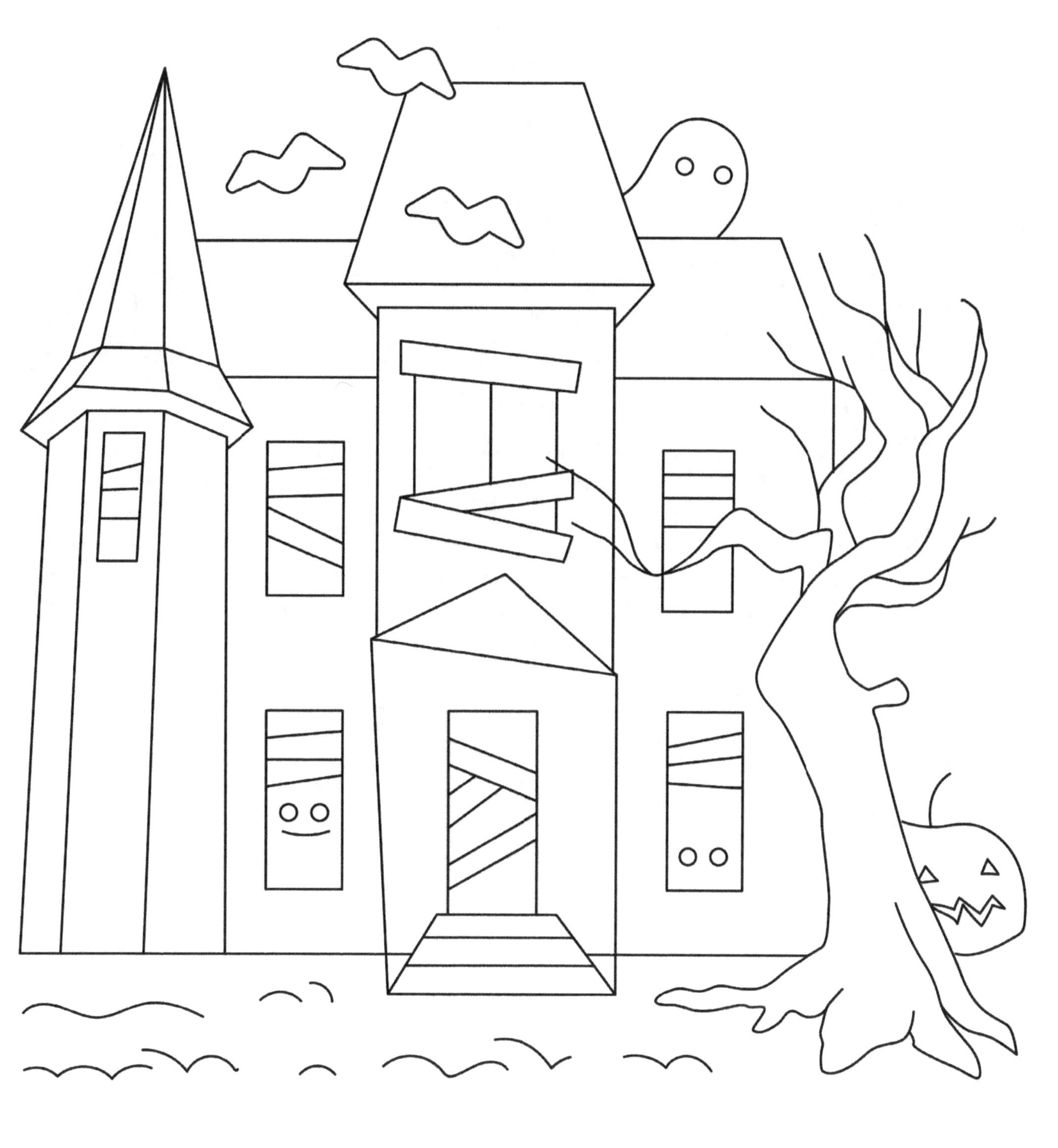

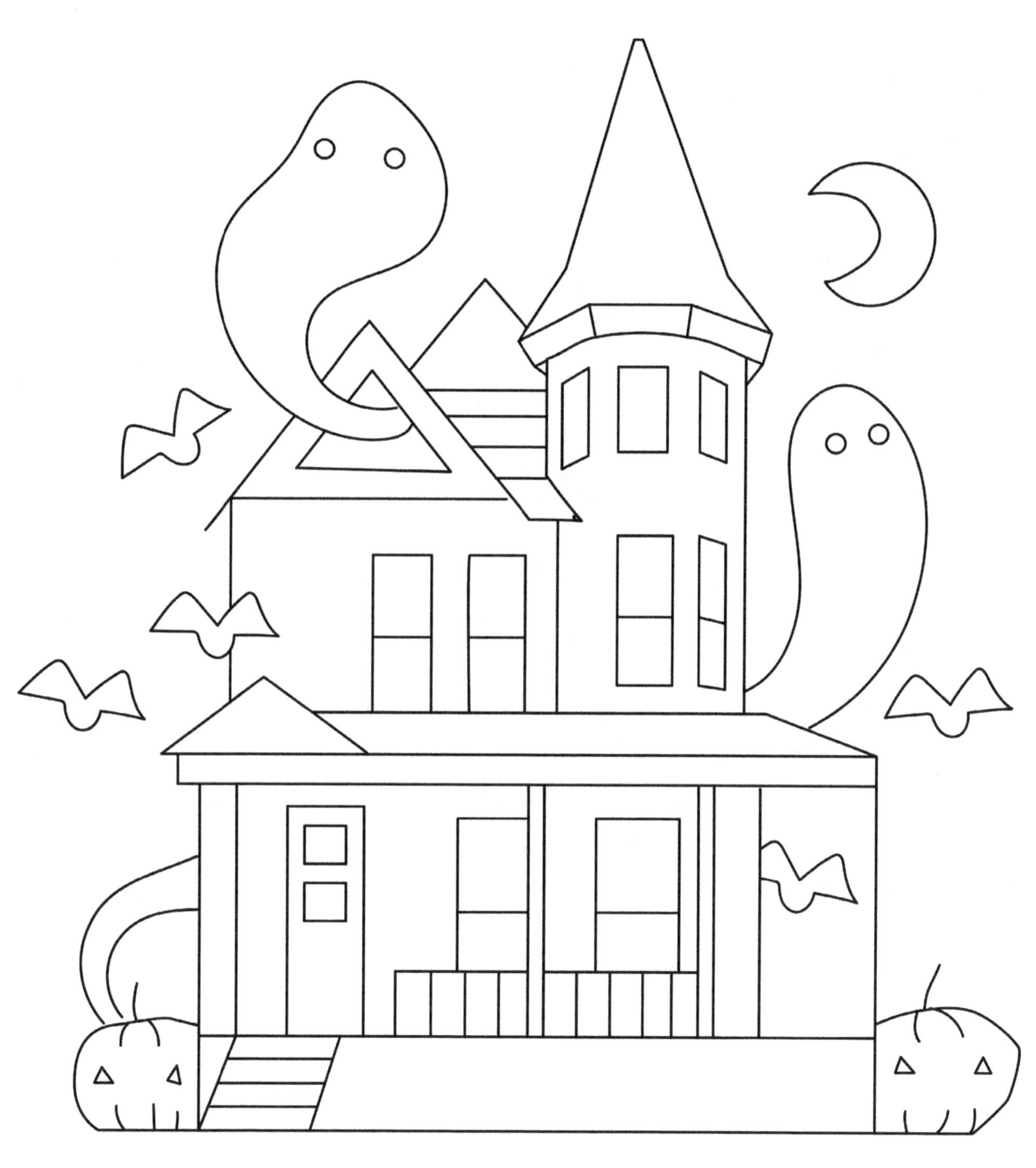

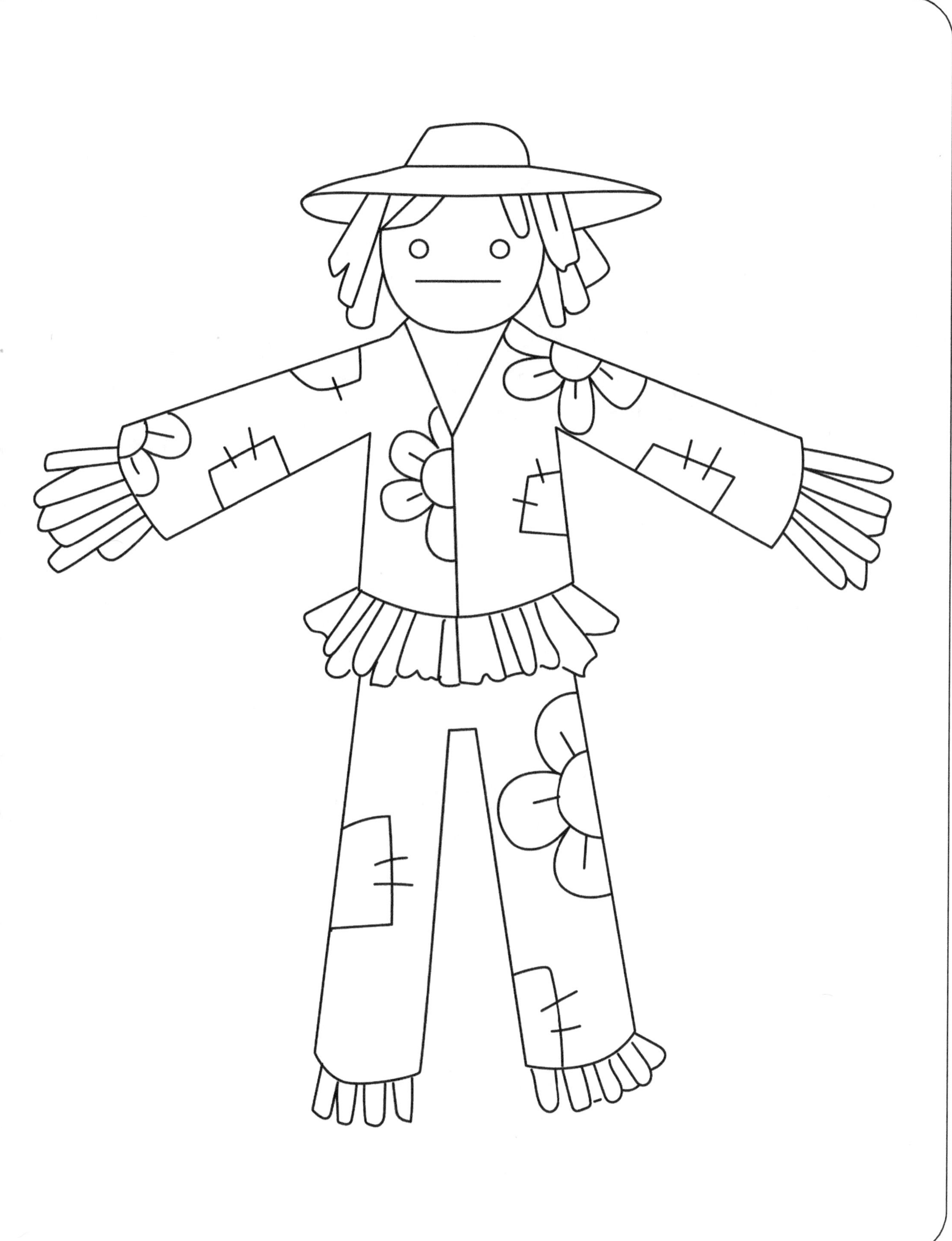